1000+ Prompts for ChatGPT

1000+ Prompts for ChatGPT

Arnold Issac

Bald and Bonkers Network Academy

First Printing, 2024

ISBN: 979-8-8691-9385-8
EISBN: 979-8-8691-9386-5

CONTENTS

CONTENTS

An Introducton

In a world propelled by technology, where innovation shapes our daily lives, a remarkable tool has emerged to redefine the way we interact with artificial intelligence: ChatGPT.

1 Understanding ChatGPT

ChatGPT stands at the forefront of natural language processing, a marvel of AI engineering. Simply put, ChatGPT is a sophisticated language model developed by OpenAI. Its primary function is to generate human-like text based on the input it receives. Whether you're seeking assistance with writing, brainstorming ideas, or engaging in conversation, Chat-GPT is your trusted companion. With its vast knowledge and adaptable algorithms, ChatGPT can generate creative stories, offer insightful advice, and simulate personalities to enrich user interactions.

2. Embracing the AI Revolution

As technology continues to evolve at an exponential rate, the role of artificial intelligence in the workplace has become increasingly prominent. From automating routine tasks to enhancing decision-making processes, AI has the potential to revolutionize virtually every industry. In this era of digital transformation, familiarity with AI and its applications is no longer optional—it's imperative. As society adapts to this shift in technology, individuals must equip themselves with the skills and knowledge needed to leverage AI effectively in their professional endeavors.

3. Bridging the Gap with Bald and Bonkers Network Academy

Bald and Bonkers Network Academy is proud to present "1000+ Prompts for ChatGPT," the latest addition to our comprehensive lineup of educational resources. As a distinguished brand and imprint of Bald and Bonkers Network LLC, we are committed to empowering individuals of all backgrounds and skill levels with the tools and expertise they need to thrive in today's rapidly changing landscape. Through our curated courses, insightful books, and innovative learning platforms, we provide entrepreneurs, content creators, and enthusiasts alike with the resources to enhance their skills, unlock their creativity, and excel in their respective fields.

In the pages ahead, you'll discover a wealth of prompts and exercises meticulously crafted to inspire creativity, foster learning, and unlock the full potential of ChatGPT. Whether you're an aspiring writer, a seasoned professional, or simply curious about the capabilities of AI, we invite you to embark on this transformative journey with us.

Welcome to the future of creativity and innovation with ChatGPT and Bald and Bonkers Network Academy. Let's embark on this exciting adventure together.

ChatGPT is a revolutionary artificial intelligence (AI) model designed to understand and generate human-like text. Developed by OpenAI, a leading research organization in artificial intelligence, ChatGPT builds upon years of research and innovation in natural language processing (NLP).

History:

The journey of ChatGPT began with the inception of OpenAI in 2015, with the mission to advance AI technology in a safe and beneficial manner for humanity. Over the years, OpenAI's team of researchers and engineers worked tirelessly to push the boundaries of AI capabilities, culminating in the development of the GPT (Generative Pre-trained Transformer) series of models.

The first iteration, GPT-1, was released in 2018 and showcased impressive capabilities in text generation and comprehension. Building upon this success, subsequent versions, including GPT-2 and GPT-3, further refined the model's capabilities, demonstrating the potential for AI to generate coherent and contextually relevant text across various domains.

Development and Purpose:

The development of ChatGPT was driven by the desire to create a versatile AI model capable of understanding and responding to human language with a high degree of fluency and coherence. By leveraging large-scale datasets and advanced machine learning techniques, the researchers at OpenAI aimed to create a model that could mimic human-like conversation and provide valuable assistance in a wide range of applications.

Various Uses:

ChatGPT has found applications across diverse domains, ranging from customer service and virtual assistants to creative writing and educational tools. Some of the key uses of ChatGPT include:

- ***Conversational Agents:*** ChatGPT powers virtual assistants and chatbots deployed by businesses to engage with customers, answer queries, and provide support round-the-clock.
- ***Content Generation:*** Writers, bloggers, and content creators use ChatGPT to generate ideas, brainstorm topics, and even assist in drafting articles, stories, and scripts.
- ***Language Translation:*** ChatGPT can aid in language translation by converting text from one language to another while preserving context and meaning.
- ***Educational Tools:*** ChatGPT serves as an educational resource, helping students with homework,

providing explanations, and offering learning support in various subjects

- ***Creative Projects:*** Artists, designers, and filmmakers leverage ChatGPT for inspiration and idea generation in creative projects, such as generating artwork descriptions, story outlines, or even dialogue for characters.

Conclusion:

In summary, ChatGPT represents a significant advancement in AI technology, enabling machines to understand and generate human-like text with remarkable accuracy and fluency. With its wide-ranging applications and potential to enhance productivity and creativity across various domains, ChatGPT continues to shape the future of human-machine interaction and pave the way for new possibilities in AI-driven innovation.

1

Advertising Prompts

1. **Copywriting: Assisting with crafting compelling advertising copy for various platforms, such as print ads, billboards, radio scripts, or digital campaigns.**
   a. [Product/Service Name]: Describe the key benefits and features of this product/service in a way that will captivate audiences on [Platform]. Incorporate a strong call-to-action that encourages potential customers to take the next step.
   b. [Target Audience]: Write a compelling [Platform] ad copy that speaks directly to the pain points and desires of our target audience, positioning [Product/Service Name] as the ultimate solution. Use persuasive language and compelling visuals to make a strong impression.
   c. [Unique Selling Proposition]: Craft an engaging [Platform] ad copy that highlights the unique selling proposition of [Product/Service Name],

distinguishing it from competitors and showcasing why it is the best choice for customers. Include a memorable tagline or slogan to reinforce the brand message.

d. [Testimonial/Case Study]: Create an authentic [Platform] ad copy featuring a customer testimonial or case study that demonstrates the real-life benefits and success stories of using [Product/Service Name]. Ensure the copy is relatable and genuine, resonating with potential customers.

e. [Limited-Time Offer]: Write a persuasive [Platform] ad copy promoting a limited-time offer or sale for [Product/Service Name]. Generate a sense of urgency that compels potential customers to act now to take advantage of the special deal, and include specific details about the offer and its expiration date.

f. [Emotional Appeal]: Develop a powerful [Platform] ad copy that evokes a strong emotional response from potential customers, such as happiness, nostalgia, or excitement. Use storytelling techniques to connect with the target audience and showcase the positive impact [Product/Service Name] can have on their lives.

g. [Seasonal Campaign]: Create a festive and eye-catching [Platform] ad copy for a seasonal campaign related to [Holiday/Event]. Incorporate seasonal imagery, themes, and messaging to make

[Product/Service Name] a must-have during this time of year.

h. [Problem-Solution]: Write a compelling [Platform] ad copy that presents a common problem faced by the target audience and positions [Product/Service Name] as the ideal solution. Use clear and concise language to illustrate how the product/service effectively addresses the issue.

i. [Contest/Giveaway]: Craft an engaging [Platform] ad copy announcing a contest or giveaway for [Product/Service Name]. Highlight the exciting prizes and rewards, and provide clear instructions on how potential customers can enter for a chance to win. Generate buzz and excitement around the brand.

j. [Cross-Promotion]: Develop a creative [Platform] ad copy that features a collaboration or partnership between [Product/Service Name] and another brand, product, or influencer. Showcase the synergistic benefits of the partnership and explain how it provides added value to the target audience.

2. **Graphic Design: Providing guidance on design principles, color theory, typography, and layout techniques to create visually appealing and effective advertisements.**

a. [Design Objective]: Provide guidance on design principles and layout techniques to create a visually appealing and effective advertisement for [Product/Service Name] on [Platform]. Consider the target audience and brand identity when suggesting design elements.

b. [Color Palette]: Recommend a color palette for an advertisement promoting [Product/Service Name] on [Platform], keeping in mind the target audience, brand identity, and psychological effects of color. Explain the reasoning behind your color choices.

c. [Typography]: Suggest appropriate typography styles and font pairings for an advertisement featuring [Product/Service Name] on [Platform]. Consider readability, visual hierarchy, and consistency with brand guidelines when making your recommendations.

d. [Hierarchy & Layout]: Provide guidance on organizing the visual elements in an advertisement for [Product/Service Name] on [Platform]. Explain how to establish a clear hierarchy and create a balanced layout that effectively communicates the intended message.

e. [Imagery & Graphics]: Offer suggestions for selecting and incorporating impactful imagery and graphics into an advertisement for [Product/Service Name] on [Platform]. Discuss the importance of visual consistency and relevance to the overall design concept.

f. [Design Trends]: Analyze current design trends

and suggest how to incorporate relevant and modern design elements into an advertisement for [Product/Service Name] on [Platform]. Describe the potential benefits and drawbacks of using trendy design elements in advertising.

g. [Accessibility]: Provide recommendations on making an advertisement for [Product/Service Name] on [Platform] more accessible to diverse audiences. Consider factors such as color contrast, font sizes, and alternative text to ensure the ad is inclusive and easily understood by all viewers.

h. [Brand Consistency]: Offer guidance on maintaining brand consistency throughout the design of an advertisement for [Product/Service Name] on [Platform]. Explain the importance of aligning the ad's visual elements with the brand's identity, tone, and messaging.

i. [Call-to-Action]: Suggest effective call-to-action (CTA) design strategies for an advertisement promoting [Product/Service Name] on [Platform]. Discuss the importance of CTA placement, visibility, and design to encourage audience engagement and conversion.

j. [Design Evaluation]: Review the design of an advertisement for [Product/Service Name] on [Platform] and provide constructive feedback. Highlight areas of improvement, such as color choices, typography, layout, and visual hierarchy, to create a more appealing and effective ad.

3. **Social Media Advertising: Offering insights into best practices for creating and managing ad campaigns on social media platforms, such as Facebook, Instagram, LinkedIn, and Twitter.**

   a. [Platform Specifics]: Explain the best practices for creating and managing ad campaigns for [Product/Service Name] on [Social Media Platform]. Offer insights on platform-specific requirements, ad formats, and targeting options to maximize campaign effectiveness.

   b. [Targeting Strategy]: Recommend a targeting strategy for an ad campaign promoting [Product/Service Name] on [Social Media Platform]. Consider factors such as demographics, interests, and behaviors to reach the most relevant audience.

   c. [Ad Formats]: Discuss the various ad formats available on [Social Media Platform] and suggest the most effective format(s) for promoting [Product/Service Name]. Explain the benefits and limitations of each format and how they can be used to achieve specific campaign objectives.

   d. [Budget & Bidding]: Provide guidance on setting and optimizing the budget and bidding strategy for an ad campaign featuring [Product/Service Name] on [Social Media Platform]. Explain how to allocate resources effectively and maximize return on ad spend (ROAS).

e. [Ad Creative]: Offer best practices for creating visually engaging and persuasive ad creatives for [Product/Service Name] on [Social Media Platform]. Discuss the importance of relevance, consistency, and a clear call-to-action to improve ad performance.

f. [Testing & Optimization]: Suggest an approach for testing and optimizing ad campaigns for [Product/Service Name] on [Social Media Platform]. Explain the importance of A/B testing, key performance indicators (KPIs), and making data-driven decisions to enhance campaign results.

g. [Campaign Measurement]: Recommend tools and techniques for measuring the success of a social media ad campaign promoting [Product/Service Name] on [Social Media Platform]. Discuss the most important metrics to track and how to interpret campaign performance data.

h. [Retargeting Strategy]: Provide insights into implementing an effective retargeting strategy for [Product/Service Name] on [Social Media Platform]. Explain the benefits of retargeting and suggest methods for refining audience segments and ad creatives to boost conversions.

i. [Organic & Paid Synergy]: Discuss the benefits of integrating organic and paid social media strategies for [Product/Service Name] on [Social Media Platform]. Offer suggestions for leveraging organic content to support paid campaigns and vice versa, creating a cohesive brand presence.

j. [Competitor Analysis]: Provide guidance on conducting a competitor analysis for social media advertising campaigns related to [Product/Service Name] on [Social Media Platform]. Discuss the importance of understanding competitor strategies, creative approaches, and targeting methods to inform your own campaign decisions and differentiate your brand.

4. **Advertising Strategy: Discussing the development of strategic advertising plans, including target audience analysis, setting campaign goals, and selecting appropriate channels.**

a. [Target Audience Analysis]: Provide guidance on conducting a comprehensive target audience analysis for an advertising campaign promoting [Product/Service Name]. Discuss the importance of understanding demographics, psychographics, and behaviors to create tailored advertising messages.

b. [Campaign Goals]: Offer suggestions for setting clear, measurable, and realistic campaign goals for an advertising campaign featuring [Product/Service Name]. Explain how these goals align with overall business objectives and help guide strategic decision-making.

c. [Channel Selection]: Recommend appropriate advertising channels for promoting [Product/

Service Name], considering factors such as target audience, budget, and campaign objectives. Discuss the pros and cons of each channel and their potential impact on campaign success.

d. [Message Development]: Provide insights on crafting persuasive and relevant advertising messages for [Product/Service Name] that resonate with the target audience. Explain how to incorporate emotional appeals, unique selling propositions, and clear calls-to-action.

e. [Media Planning & Buying]: Discuss the process of media planning and buying for an advertising campaign featuring [Product/Service Name]. Offer guidance on negotiating media placements, optimizing reach and frequency, and allocating budget effectively.

f. [Integrated Marketing Communications]: Explain the importance of integrating advertising efforts across multiple channels and platforms for [Product/Service Name]. Offer suggestions for creating a cohesive, consistent, and impactful brand presence that maximizes campaign effectiveness.

g. [Competitive Analysis]: Provide guidance on conducting a competitive analysis to inform the advertising strategy for [Product/Service Name]. Discuss the importance of understanding competitor positioning, messaging, and tactics to differentiate your brand and gain a competitive edge.

h. [Content Strategy]: Offer insights on developing a content strategy for an advertising campaign promoting [Product/Service Name]. Explain how to align content with target audience preferences, campaign goals, and channel requirements to create engaging and effective ad creatives.

i. [Campaign Timeline]: Recommend a timeline for planning, launching, and monitoring an advertising campaign for [Product/Service Name]. Discuss the importance of setting milestones and deadlines to ensure the smooth execution of campaign tasks and activities.

j. [Campaign Evaluation]: Provide guidance on establishing a framework for evaluating the success of an advertising campaign for [Product/Service Name]. Discuss the importance of setting key performance indicators (KPIs) and using data-driven insights to refine campaign strategies and tactics.

5. **Advertising Analytics: Explaining how to measure advertising effectiveness and ROI, and providing guidance on interpreting key performance indicators (KPIs).**

a. [KPI Selection]: Recommend the most relevant key performance indicators (KPIs) for measuring the success of an advertising campaign promoting [Product/Service Name]. Explain the importance of each KPI and how it aligns with overall campaign objectives.

b. [ROI Calculation]: Explain how to calculate return on investment (ROI) for an advertising campaign featuring [Product/Service Name]. Discuss the factors to consider when determining campaign costs, revenue, and overall profitability.

c. [Data Collection]: Offer guidance on setting up data collection and tracking for an advertising campaign promoting [Product/Service Name]. Discuss the tools and techniques for capturing accurate and reliable performance data.

d. [Data Analysis]: Provide insights on analyzing advertising campaign data to measure effectiveness and inform decision-making for [Product/Service Name]. Explain how to identify trends, patterns, and areas for improvement using performance data.

e. [A/B Testing]: Discuss the importance of A/B testing in advertising analytics for [Product/Service Name]. Offer suggestions for designing and executing effective tests to optimize ad creatives, targeting, and messaging.

f. [Conversion Attribution]: Explain the concept of conversion attribution and its importance in measuring the success of an advertising campaign for [Product/Service Name]. Discuss different attribution models and suggest the most appropriate model(s) to accurately attribute conversions to specific ad efforts.

g. [Optimization Strategies]: Offer guidance on using advertising analytics data to optimize campaign performance for [Product/Service Name]. Discuss strategies for improving targeting, creative elements, and media placements to enhance overall campaign effectiveness.

h. [Dashboard & Reporting]: Recommend best practices for creating a comprehensive advertising analytics dashboard and reporting system for [Product/Service Name]. Explain how to visualize and communicate campaign performance data in a clear and actionable manner.

i. [Benchmarking]: Provide insights on benchmarking the performance of an advertising campaign for [Product/Service Name] against industry standards and competitor campaigns. Discuss the importance of understanding relative performance to identify areas of strength and weakness.

j. [Continuous Improvement]: Discuss the concept of continuous improvement in advertising analytics and its importance for [Product/Service Name]. Offer suggestions for leveraging data-driven insights to refine and enhance advertising strategies and tactics over time.

6. **Search Engine Advertising: Offering advice on creating and optimizing pay-per-click (PPC) cam-**

paigns for search engines like Google Ads and Bing Ads.

a. [Keyword Research]: Provide guidance on conducting comprehensive keyword research for a PPC campaign promoting [Product/Service Name]. Discuss the importance of identifying relevant, high-intent keywords and understanding search volume and competition.

b. [Campaign Structure]: Offer recommendations for organizing a search engine advertising campaign for [Product/Service Name]. Explain how to create effective ad groups, keyword groupings, and ad variations to maximize campaign performance.

c. [Ad Copywriting]: Provide best practices for writing compelling and relevant ad copy for a PPC campaign featuring [Product/Service Name]. Discuss the importance of incorporating keywords, clear calls-to-action, and unique selling propositions.

d. [Quality Score]: Explain the concept of Quality Score in search engine advertising and its impact on [Product/Service Name]'s PPC campaign. Offer suggestions for improving Quality Score to lower cost-per-click (CPC) and increase ad visibility.

e. [Bidding Strategy]: Discuss various bidding strategies for a PPC campaign promoting [Product/Service Name] and recommend the most suitable approach based on campaign objectives, budget, and competition.

f. [Ad Extensions]: Offer insights on using ad extensions to enhance PPC ads for [Product/Service Name]. Explain the benefits of different extension types and how they can improve ad performance by providing additional information and calls-to-action.

g. [Landing Page Optimization]: Provide guidance on optimizing landing pages for a search engine advertising campaign promoting [Product/Service Name]. Discuss the importance of relevance, user experience, and clear conversion paths to improve campaign success.

h. [Negative Keywords]: Explain the role of negative keywords in a PPC campaign for [Product/Service Name] and offer guidance on identifying and implementing negative keywords to refine targeting and reduce wasted ad spend.

i. [Performance Monitoring]: Recommend best practices for monitoring and analyzing the performance of a search engine advertising campaign for [Product/Service Name]. Discuss the importance of tracking key performance indicators (KPIs), adjusting bids, and optimizing ad copy and landing pages based on data-driven insights.

j. [Remarketing]: Provide insights on implementing an effective remarketing strategy for a PPC campaign featuring [Product/Service Name]. Discuss the benefits of remarketing and suggest methods for refining audience segments and ad creatives to boost conversions.

7. **Native Advertising: Providing insights into the creation and implementation of native advertising campaigns, including sponsored content and in-feed ads that blend seamlessly with a platform's user experience.**

   a. [Native Ad Formats]: Discuss the various native advertising formats available for promoting [Product/Service Name] and recommend the most suitable format(s) based on campaign objectives and target audience preferences.

   b. [Platform Selection]: Offer guidance on selecting the most appropriate platform(s) for a native advertising campaign featuring [Product/Service Name]. Consider factors such as audience demographics, content consumption habits, and platform user experience.

   c. [Content Creation]: Provide best practices for creating engaging and relevant native ad content for [Product/Service Name]. Discuss the importance of storytelling, providing value, and aligning with the platform's content style.

   d. [Sponsored Content]: Offer insights on creating sponsored content that seamlessly integrates with a platform's editorial content for [Product/Service Name]. Explain how to balance promotional messaging with valuable information to engage and inform the target audience.

e. [Disclosure & Transparency]: Discuss the importance of disclosure and transparency in native advertising for [Product/Service Name]. Provide guidance on adhering to regulatory requirements and maintaining audience trust.

f. [Targeting & Personalization]: Recommend targeting and personalization strategies for a native advertising campaign promoting [Product/Service Name]. Discuss the benefits of delivering tailored content to specific audience segments.

g. [Performance Metrics]: Suggest the most relevant performance metrics for measuring the success of a native advertising campaign for [Product/Service Name]. Explain the importance of each metric and how it aligns with overall campaign objectives.

h. [Optimization]: Offer guidance on optimizing native advertising campaigns for [Product/Service Name] based on performance data. Discuss strategies for refining content, targeting, and distribution to enhance overall campaign effectiveness and ROI.

i. [Content Amplification]: Provide insights on leveraging content amplification techniques to boost the reach and visibility of native advertising content for [Product/Service Name]. Discuss the use of social media, influencer partnerships, and paid promotion to drive engagement and conversions.

   j. [Native Advertising Trends]: Analyze current native advertising trends and suggest how to incorporate relevant and innovative approaches into a campaign for [Product/Service Name]. Describe the potential benefits and drawbacks of using trending tactics in native advertising.

8. **Influencer Marketing: Discussing the use of influencers and content creators for advertising purposes, including collaboration strategies, budgeting, and measuring campaign success.**

   a. [Influencer Selection]: Offer guidance on selecting the right influencers for an influencer marketing campaign promoting [Product/Service Name]. Discuss factors such as audience demographics, engagement rates, and content alignment to ensure a successful partnership.

   b. [Collaboration Strategies]: Recommend effective collaboration strategies for working with influencers to promote [Product/Service Name]. Discuss options such as sponsored posts, giveaways, and product reviews, and explain the benefits of each approach.

   c. [Campaign Budgeting]: Provide insights on budgeting for an influencer marketing campaign featuring [Product/Service Name]. Discuss factors to consider when allocating resources, such as influencer fees, content production costs, and promotional expenses.

d. [Influencer Brief]: Offer suggestions for creating a comprehensive influencer brief that outlines the objectives, key messages, and guidelines for a campaign promoting [Product/Service Name]. Explain the importance of clear communication and setting expectations with influencers.

e. [Content Approval]: Discuss the process of reviewing and approving influencer-created content for a campaign featuring [Product/Service Name]. Offer guidance on maintaining brand consistency while allowing influencers creative freedom to engage their audiences authentically.

f. [Campaign Timeline]: Recommend a timeline for planning, executing, and evaluating an influencer marketing campaign for [Product/Service Name]. Discuss the importance of setting milestones and deadlines to ensure smooth collaboration and timely content delivery.

g. [Influencer Contracts]: Provide guidance on drafting influencer contracts for a campaign promoting [Product/Service Name]. Discuss key elements to include, such as deliverables, payment terms, and content usage rights.

h. [Campaign Monitoring]: Offer best practices for monitoring and managing an influencer marketing campaign for [Product/Service Name]. Discuss the importance of tracking performance metrics, maintaining communication, and addressing any issues that may arise.

i. [Measuring Success]: Recommend the most relevant key performance indicators (KPIs) for measuring the success of an influencer marketing campaign promoting [Product/Service Name]. Explain the importance of each KPI and how it aligns with overall campaign objectives.

j. [Influencer Collaboration and Brand Alignment]: Explore the process of selecting the right influencers for a marketing campaign promoting [Product/Service Name]. Dive into the importance of brand alignment, audience demographics, engagement metrics, and the influencer's content aesthetics. Additionally, discuss strategies to foster genuine partnerships, ensuring that collaborations are both authentic and effective in resonating with the target audience. Highlight potential pitfalls and offer best practices for maximizing ROI through seamless influencer integrations.

9. **Video Advertising: Offering guidance on creating impactful video ads, including scriptwriting, production techniques, and platform-specific considerations.**

a. [Scriptwriting]: Offer best practices for writing an engaging and persuasive script for a video ad promoting [Product/Service Name]. Discuss the importance of storytelling, emotional appeals, and clear calls-to-action.

b. [Video Production Techniques]: Provide guidance on effective video production techniques for creating impactful ads featuring [Product/Service Name]. Discuss aspects such as lighting, camera angles, and editing to enhance the overall visual appeal and message clarity.

c. [Platform-Specific Considerations]: Recommend platform-specific considerations for creating video ads promoting [Product/Service Name] on platforms like YouTube, Facebook, and Instagram. Discuss factors such as video length, aspect ratio, and user behavior.

d. [Video Ad Formats]: Discuss the various video ad formats available for promoting [Product/Service Name] and recommend the most suitable format(s) based on campaign objectives and target audience preferences.

e. [Video Ad Targeting]: Offer insights on targeting strategies for video advertising campaigns featuring [Product/Service Name]. Explain the importance of demographic, geographic, and behavioral targeting to reach the most relevant audience.

f. [Budgeting & Bidding]: Provide guidance on budgeting and bidding for a video advertising campaign promoting [Product/Service Name]. Discuss factors such as cost-per-view (CPV), cost-per-click (CPC), and cost-per-thousand-impressions (CPM) to optimize ad spend.

g. [Ad Performance Metrics]: Suggest the most relevant performance metrics for measuring the success of a video advertising campaign for [Product/Service Name]. Explain the importance of each metric and how it aligns with overall campaign objectives.

h. [A/B Testing]: Discuss the importance of A/B testing in video advertising for [Product/Service Name]. Offer suggestions for designing and executing effective tests to optimize ad creatives, targeting, and messaging.

i. [Video Ad Optimization]: Provide insights on using performance data to optimize video advertising campaigns for [Product/Service Name]. Discuss strategies for refining targeting, creative elements, and bidding to enhance overall campaign effectiveness and ROI.

j. [Video Ad Trends]: Analyze current video advertising trends and suggest how to incorporate relevant and innovative approaches into a campaign for [Product/Service Name]. Describe the potential benefits and drawbacks of using trending tactics in video advertising.

10. **Advertising Ethics and Regulations: Explaining the ethical considerations and regulatory requirements surrounding advertising, such as truth-in-**

advertising laws, privacy concerns, and industry-specific guidelines.

a. [Misleading Claims]: Identify potential misleading claims in the advertising campaign for [Product/Service Name] and suggest ways to ensure compliance with truth-in-advertising regulations. Discuss the consequences of not adhering to these regulations.

b. [Privacy Concerns]: Evaluate the privacy concerns in the proposed data collection and targeted advertising strategies for [Product/Service Name]. Recommend best practices to address these concerns while maintaining an effective marketing campaign.

c. [Industry-Specific Guidelines]: Examine the industry-specific advertising guidelines for [Product/Service Industry] and analyze how they impact the marketing campaign for [Product/Service Name]. Propose strategies to meet these guidelines without sacrificing the campaign's effectiveness.

d. [Comparative Advertising]: Discuss the ethical considerations and legal requirements of using comparative advertising for [Product/Service Name] against [Competitor's Product/Service]. Suggest ways to create a fair and accurate comparison that complies with advertising regulations.

e. [Children-targeted Ads]: Assess the ethical implications and regulatory requirements of targeting advertising for [Product/Service Name] towards children. Propose best practices to ensure responsible advertising while still reaching the intended audience.

f. [Cultural Sensitivity]: Analyze the cultural aspects of the advertising campaign for [Product/Service Name] and identify any potential ethical issues or cultural insensitivities. Offer recommendations for creating a more inclusive and culturally sensitive campaign.

g. [Endorsements and Testimonials]: Investigate the ethical concerns and regulatory guidelines surrounding the use of endorsements and testimonials in advertising for [Product/Service Name]. Provide suggestions for obtaining and presenting credible and compliant endorsements.

h. [Native Advertising]: Explore the ethical considerations and regulatory requirements for using native advertising in promoting [Product/Service Name]. Propose strategies to maintain transparency and adhere to guidelines while leveraging the advantages of native advertising.

i. [Environmental Claims]: Analyze the environmental claims made in the advertising campaign for [Product/Service Name] and discuss their accuracy, potential for greenwashing, and any associated regulatory requirements. Suggest ways to improve the campaign's credibility and compliance.

j. [Influencer Marketing]: Examine the ethical issues and regulatory requirements related to influencer marketing for [Product/Service Name]. Recommend best practices for collaborating with influencers to create authentic, transparent, and compliant promotional content.

2

Content Creation Prompts

1. **Writing and Editing: Providing guidance on crafting compelling written content, such as blog posts, articles, and social media updates, as well as editing techniques to ensure clarity and polish.**
   a. [Effective Writing Techniques]: Share tips and strategies for crafting compelling written content, including writing styles, sentence structure, and tone.
   b. [Editing for Clarity and Polish]: Provide guidance on editing techniques to enhance clarity, readability, and professionalism in written content.
   c. [Grammar and Punctuation]: Offer advice on mastering grammar and punctuation rules to improve writing quality and avoid common mistakes.
   d. [Writing for Different Formats]: Discuss adapting writing styles for various formats, such as

blog posts, articles, social media updates, and email newsletters.

e. [Storytelling in Writing]: Share insights on incorporating storytelling elements into written content to engage readers and convey a clear message.

f. [Developing a Writing Routine]: Offer guidance on establishing a consistent writing routine to boost productivity and enhance creativity.

g. [Overcoming Writer's Block]: Provide strategies for overcoming writer's block and maintaining momentum during the writing process.

h. [Writing for Different Audiences]: Discuss tailoring written content to resonate with different target audiences and demographics.

i. [Collaborative Writing and Editing]: Explore best practices for working with co-authors, editors, and proofreaders to improve written content.

j. [Self-Editing Techniques]: Share tips for self-editing written content to ensure quality, consistency, and accuracy before sharing or publishing.

2. **Visual Content: Offering insights into creating eye-catching visual content, including photography, graphic design, and data visualization techniques.**

a. [Photography Techniques]: Offer guidance on capturing eye-catching photographs for use in visual content, including composition, lighting, and post-processing.

b. [Graphic Design Principles]: Discuss fundamental graphic design principles for creating visually appealing and impactful designs.

c. [Data Visualization Techniques]: Provide insights on transforming data into visually engaging and informative graphics, such as charts, graphs, and infographics.

d. [Visual Content for Social Media]: Share best practices for creating and adapting visual content for various social media platforms.

e. [Design Tools and Resources]: Offer guidance on popular design tools, software, and resources for creating visual content.

f. [Visual Branding]: Discuss the importance of visual branding in content creation and provide tips for maintaining brand consistency across various visual assets.

g. [Typography and Layout]: Explore the role of typography and layout in creating visually appealing and easy-to-read content.

h. [Color Theory and Palette Selection]: Share insights on color theory and choosing the right color palette for visual content.

i. [Visual Content Accessibility]: Provide guidance on ensuring visual content is accessible to individuals with visual impairments or other disabilities.

j. [Stock Images vs. Original Visuals]: Discuss the benefits and drawbacks of using stock images versus creating original visuals for content.

3. **Video Production: Assisting with the planning, shooting, and editing of engaging video content for various platforms, such as YouTube, Instagram, or TikTok.**

   a. [Video Planning and Scriptwriting]: Offer guidance on planning and scriptwriting for engaging video content across various platforms.

   b. [Shooting Techniques]: Share tips on shooting high-quality video footage, including camera settings, lighting, and composition.

   c. [Video Editing Tools and Techniques]: Discuss popular video editing tools and techniques to create polished, professional video content.

   d. [Adding Audio to Video]: Provide insights on incorporating audio elements, such as voiceovers, music, and sound effects, into video content.

   e. [Video Formats and Platforms]: Explore best practices for adapting video content for different formats and platforms, such as YouTube, Instagram, or TikTok.

   f. [Video Storytelling]: Share tips for incorporating storytelling elements into video content to captivate and engage viewers.

   g. [Animations and Motion Graphics]: Discuss the use of animations and motion graphics to enhance video content and convey complex information.

   h. [Video Accessibility]: Offer guidance on ensuring video content is accessible to individuals with hearing impairments or other disabilities, such as adding captions or transcripts.

i. [Collaboration in Video Production]: Explore best practices for working with videographers, editors, and other team members during the video production process.

j. [Video Content Distribution and Promotion]: Share strategies for distributing and promoting video content to reach the target audience and maximize engagement.

4. **Audio Content and Podcasting: Discussing the creation and production of high-quality audio content, including podcast planning, recording techniques, and editing tools.**

a. [Podcast Planning and Structure]: Discuss key considerations for planning and structuring a podcast, including format, episode length, and release frequency.

b. [Recording Techniques]: Offer guidance on capturing high-quality audio recordings, including equipment, microphone techniques, and sound-proofing.

c. [Audio Editing Tools and Techniques]: Share tips on using audio editing tools and techniques to create polished, professional podcast episodes.

d. [Interviewing Guests and Co-Hosts]: Provide insights on effectively interviewing podcast guests and collaborating with co-hosts to create engaging conversations.

e. [Scriptwriting for Podcasts]: Discuss the role of scriptwriting in podcast production and share tips for crafting compelling episode outlines and introductions.

f. [Podcast Promotion and Distribution]: Offer guidance on promoting and distributing podcast episodes to reach the target audience and maximize engagement.

g. [Monetizing Podcasts]: Explore strategies for monetizing a podcast, such as sponsorships, advertising, and listener-supported models.

h. [Podcast Accessibility]: Share tips for making podcasts accessible to individuals with hearing impairments or other disabilities, such as providing transcripts or captions.

i. [Creating Audiobooks and Audio Narratives]: Discuss the process of creating audiobooks or audio narratives, including narration techniques and production considerations.

j. [Building a Podcast Community]: Provide insights on fostering a sense of community among podcast listeners through engagement and interaction.

5. **Content Strategy: Providing guidance on developing a comprehensive content strategy, including content planning, audience analysis, and distribution channels.**

a. [Developing a Content Strategy]: Discuss key steps in developing a comprehensive content strategy, including goal setting, audience analysis, and content planning.

b. [Audience Analysis]: Offer guidance on identifying and understanding target audiences, including creating personas and conducting market research.

c. [Content Planning and Scheduling]: Share tips for creating a content plan and editorial calendar to organize content production and distribution.

d. [Content Formats and Channels]: Explore the various content formats and channels available, such as blog posts, social media updates, videos, and podcasts.

e. [Content Distribution]: Provide insights on effective content distribution strategies to maximize reach and engagement across multiple platforms.

f. [Measuring Content Success]: Discuss the importance of tracking content performance and key metrics to inform strategy and future content creation.

g. [Maintaining a Consistent Brand Voice]: Offer guidance on establishing and maintaining a consistent brand voice across all content channels.

h. [Content Curation]: Share tips on curating high-quality, relevant content from external sources to supplement original content and engage the audience.

i. [Collaboration in Content Strategy]: Explore

best practices for collaborating with writers, designers, videographers, and other content creators to execute a content strategy.

j. [Content Strategy Trends]: Discuss emerging trends in content strategy and how they may impact future content planning and execution.

6. **Search Engine Optimization (SEO): Offering advice on optimizing content for search engines, including keyword research, on-page optimization, and link-building techniques.**

1. [SEO Basics]: Provide an overview of the key concepts and techniques in search engine optimization for content creators.

2. [Keyword Research]: Offer guidance on conducting keyword research to identify relevant, high-traffic search terms for content optimization.

3. [On-Page Optimization]: Share tips for optimizing content elements, such as titles, headings, and meta descriptions, to improve search engine visibility.

4. [Link Building]: Discuss strategies for building high-quality inbound links to improve domain authority and search engine rankings.

5. [Technical SEO]: Explore the role of technical SEO, such as site speed, mobile-friendliness, and structured data, in content optimization.

6. [Content and SEO]: Offer guidance on creating search engine-friendly content that also appeals to the target audience.

7. [Local SEO]: Share tips for optimizing content to target local audiences and improve visibility in local search results.

8. [SEO Tools and Resources]: Discuss popular SEO tools and resources to assist content creators with keyword research, on-page optimization, and performance tracking.

9. [SEO Best Practices]: Provide insights on staying up-to-date with search engine algorithm updates and adhering to SEO best practices.

10. [Measuring SEO Success]: Offer guidance on tracking the impact of SEO efforts on content performance, rankings, and organic traffic.

7. **Social Media Content: Exploring best practices for creating engaging and shareable content across various social media platforms, such as Facebook, Twitter, LinkedIn, and Pinterest.**

   a. [Creating Engaging Social Media Content]: Discuss the key elements of engaging social media content and best practices for different platforms.

   b. [Visual Content for Social Media]: Offer guidance on creating eye-catching visual content for social media, including images, videos, and GIFs.

   c. [Optimizing Content for Social Platforms]: Share tips for tailoring content to specific social media platforms, such as Facebook, Twitter, LinkedIn, and Instagram.

   d. [Social Media Content Planning]: Discuss strategies for planning and scheduling social media content to maintain a consistent online presence.

e. [Hashtags and Social Media]: Explore the use of hashtags to increase content visibility and engage with targeted audiences on social media platforms.

f. [Building a Social Media Community]: Offer guidance on fostering engagement and building a loyal community on social media through content and interaction.

g. [User-Generated Content]: Share tips on leveraging user-generated content to enhance social media marketing efforts and build brand authenticity.

h. [Social Media Analytics]: Discuss the importance of tracking social media content performance and using insights to inform future content creation.

i. [Social Media Content Trends]: Explore emerging trends in social media content and how they may impact content creation strategies.

j. [Social Media Advertising]: Provide insights on using paid social media advertising to boost content visibility and reach a wider audience.

8. **Content Analytics: Discussing the importance of analyzing content performance, including key metrics, engagement data, and using insights to inform content strategy.**

a. [Importance of Content Analytics]: Discuss the

significance of analyzing content performance and how it can inform future content creation and strategy.

b. [Key Content Metrics]: Offer guidance on identifying and tracking key content performance metrics, such as page views, engagement rates, and conversions.

c. [Analyzing Audience Behavior]: Share tips for analyzing audience behavior, including user demographics, browsing patterns, and content preferences.

d. [Using Google Analytics]: Provide insights on using Google Analytics to track content performance and gather valuable audience data.

e. [Content A/B Testing]: Discuss the use of A/B testing to compare different content variations and determine which performs best.

f. [Competitive Analysis]: Offer guidance on conducting competitive content analysis to identify gaps, opportunities, and best practices.

g. [Content ROI]: Share tips for measuring content return on investment (ROI) and evaluating the effectiveness of content marketing efforts.

h. [Social Media Analytics]: Explore the role of social media analytics in tracking content performance and audience engagement.

i. [Improving Content Performance]: Provide insights on using content analytics data to optimize content for better performance and audience satisfaction.

    j. [Content Analytics Tools]: Discuss popular content analytics tools and platforms that can assist with tracking and analyzing content performance.

9. **Content Repurposing: Providing guidance on repurposing existing content into new formats or for different platforms to maximize reach and engagement.**

    a. [Benefits of Content Repurposing]: Discuss the advantages of repurposing existing content into new formats or for different platforms.

    b. [Identifying Content for Repurposing]: Offer guidance on selecting high-performing or evergreen content suitable for repurposing.

    c. [Transforming Blog Posts]: Share tips for repurposing blog posts into different formats, such as infographics, videos, or social media updates.

    d. [Repurposing Video Content]: Explore strategies for repurposing video content, such as creating shorter clips or extracting audio for podcasts.

    e. [Turning Presentations into Content]: Discuss how to repurpose presentations or slides into blog posts, articles, or social media updates.

    f. [Repurposing for Different Audiences]: Offer guidance on adapting content for different target audiences or customer segments.

    g. [Leveraging User-Generated Content]: Share tips

for repurposing user-generated content to engage audiences and build brand authenticity.

h. [Repurposing for SEO]: Discuss the benefits of repurposing content for search engine optimization and improving organic visibility.

i. [Content Syndication]: Offer insights into content syndication strategies, including republishing content on different platforms to reach a wider audience.

j. [Maximizing Content Lifespan]: Discuss best practices for updating and repurposing evergreen content to maintain relevance and extend its lifespan.

10. **Content Marketing: Exploring the role of content creation in content marketing, including inbound marketing strategies, lead generation, and building brand awareness.**

a. [Content Marketing Fundamentals]: Explore the role of content creation in content marketing and the importance of creating valuable, relevant content for target audiences.

b. [Inbound Marketing Strategies]: Discuss how content creation supports inbound marketing efforts, attracting potential customers and building brand awareness.

c. [Content Marketing for Lead Generation]: Offer guidance on creating content that generates leads, including blog posts, whitepapers, and webinars.

d. [Building a Content Marketing Strategy]: Share

tips for developing a comprehensive content marketing strategy, including audience analysis, content planning, and distribution channels.

e. [Content Distribution]: Explore best practices for distributing content across various channels, such as social media, email marketing, and guest blogging.

f. [Content Marketing KPIs]: Discuss the key performance indicators (KPIs) to track and measure the success of content marketing efforts.

g. [Content Marketing and SEO]: Offer insights into optimizing content for search engines as part of a content marketing strategy.

h. [Storytelling in Content Marketing]: Share tips for using storytelling techniques to create engaging and memorable content that resonates with audiences.

i. [User-Generated Content in Marketing]: Discuss the role of user-generated content in content marketing and strategies for encouraging and leveraging it.

j. [Content Marketing Trends]: Explore emerging trends in content marketing and their potential impact on content creation and strategy.

3

Copywriting Prompts

1. **Headline Writing: Providing guidance on crafting attention-grabbing headlines that effectively convey the core message and entice readers to engage with the content.**
   a. Attention-Grabbing Headlines: Share your best tips and tricks for creating headlines that grab readers' attention, no matter the topic or industry. Emphasize the importance of using powerful language, playing with different lengths, and considering the target audience.
   b. Crafting Headlines for Social Media: Offer advice on crafting effective headlines specifically for social media platforms like Facebook, Twitter, and Instagram. Discuss how to make headlines stand out in a crowded feed, including using emojis, incorporating hashtags, and leveraging trending topics.

c. The Power of Numbers in Headlines: Explain why headlines that include numbers tend to perform better than those that don't. Share your top strategies for incorporating numbers into headlines, such as using odd numbers, making lists, and including specific statistics.

d. Writing Headlines that Appeal to Emotions: Discuss the importance of emotional appeal in headlines and how to craft headlines that tap into readers' emotions. Touch on key emotions like fear, joy, curiosity, and urgency, and provide examples of headlines that successfully tap into these emotions.

e. How to Write Headlines for SEO: Describe the key considerations for writing headlines that are optimized for search engines. Discuss the importance of including relevant keywords, keeping headlines under a certain length, and making headlines unique and descriptive.

f. Creating Headlines that Tell a Story: Share your insights on how to craft headlines that tell a compelling story and entice readers to engage with the content. Offer tips on using specific language, adding intrigue, and foreshadowing the content of the article.

g. The Art of the Clickbait Headline: Explore the controversial topic of clickbait headlines, sharing the pros and cons of this style and when it might be appropriate to use it. Discuss the line between effective clickbait and misleading headlines, and provide examples of both.

h. Writing Headlines for Different Content Formats: Discuss how to craft headlines that work well for different types of content, including blog posts, videos, and podcasts. Emphasize the importance of tailoring headlines to the specific medium and audience.

i. Headline Writing for Branding: Explain how headlines can be used to build a brand and convey its core messaging. Offer strategies for incorporating brand keywords, tone, and messaging into headlines, as well as using headlines to position the brand in the marketplace.

j. Headline Mistakes to Avoid: Share common headline mistakes that can turn readers off and prevent them from engaging with content. Discuss issues like misleading language, overused clickbait tactics, and lack of clarity or specificity, and offer tips for avoiding these mistakes.

2. **Ad Copywriting: Offering insights into creating persuasive ad copy for various advertising mediums, such as print, digital, radio, and television.**

a. The Art of Persuasive Ad Copy: Share your insights on how to create ad copy that is persuasive and compelling across different mediums. Offer tips on using language that resonates with the target audience, focusing on benefits rather than features, and using persuasive elements like social proof and scarcity.

b. Writing Ad Copy for Print Media: Describe the key considerations for writing effective ad copy for print media like newspapers, magazines, and billboards. Discuss the importance of brevity, using eye-catching visuals, and making the copy easy to read at a glance.

c. Creating Ad Copy for Digital Ads: Offer guidance on crafting ad copy for digital advertising channels like Google Ads and Facebook Ads. Discuss how to tailor the copy to the platform and audience, using attention-grabbing headlines and concise, benefit-driven language.

d. Radio Ad Copywriting: Describe the unique challenges and opportunities of writing ad copy for radio, where visuals cannot be relied upon. Discuss how to create ad copy that is attention-grabbing, memorable, and easily understood by listeners.

e. Television Ad Copy: Explore the key elements of successful television ad copy, including using visual and auditory cues to convey emotion and the importance of creating a clear, memorable message.

f. Creating Ad Copy for Social Media: Offer guidance on how to craft ad copy that effectively engages users on social media platforms like Facebook, Instagram, and Twitter. Discuss the importance of using conversational language, targeting the right audience, and including a strong call-to-action.

g. The Power of Emotional Appeal in Ad Copy: Discuss the importance of appealing to emotions in ad copy and offer tips on how to do so effectively. Touch on key emotions like fear, joy, curiosity, and urgency and provide examples of ads that successfully tap into these emotions.

h. Ad Copy for Branding: Describe how ad copy can be used to build a brand and convey its core messaging. Offer strategies for incorporating brand keywords, tone, and messaging into ad copy, as well as using ads to position the brand in the marketplace.

i. Writing Ad Copy that Sells: Share your best tips and tricks for creating ad copy that is persuasive and effective at driving sales. Discuss how to highlight benefits, address objections, and make a compelling call-to-action.

j. Ad Copy Mistakes to Avoid: Share common ad copy mistakes that can turn readers off and prevent them from engaging with the ad. Discuss issues like using cliches, lack of specificity, and not focusing on the target audience, and offer tips for avoiding these mistakes.

3. **Direct Response Copywriting: Discussing strategies for crafting compelling direct response copy that**

encourages immediate action, such as purchasing a product or signing up for a newsletter.

a. Writing Effective Direct Response Copy: Share your insights on how to create direct response copy that effectively encourages immediate action. Offer tips on using benefit-driven language, including social proof and urgency, and making a strong call-to-action.

b. Crafting Headlines for Direct Response Copy: Discuss the importance of crafting attention-grabbing headlines for direct response copy and provide examples of successful headlines. Touch on key strategies like using numbers, creating a sense of urgency, and highlighting benefits.

c. The Power of Emotional Appeal in Direct Response Copy: Explain how to effectively tap into emotions in direct response copy, such as fear, joy, curiosity, and urgency. Offer tips on how to use language that resonates with the target audience and motivates them to take action.

d. Writing Direct Response Copy for Landing Pages: Offer guidance on crafting direct response copy for landing pages that effectively converts visitors into leads or customers. Discuss how to make the copy concise, benefit-driven, and include a clear call-to-action.

e. Direct Response Copy for Email Marketing: Describe the key considerations for writing effective direct response copy for email marketing campaigns. Discuss the importance of crafting attention-grabbing subject lines, using personalization, and creating a sense of urgency.

f. Creating Direct Response Copy for Sales Pages: Discuss the unique challenges and opportunities of writing direct response copy for sales pages. Touch on key strategies like using persuasive language, addressing objections, and creating a sense of scarcity.

g. Writing Direct Response Copy for Social Media: Offer guidance on how to craft direct response copy for social media platforms like Facebook, Twitter, and Instagram. Discuss how to use benefit-driven language, creating a sense of urgency, and using strong calls-to-action.

h. Direct Response Copy for Free Offers: Describe the key elements of successful direct response copy for free offers like lead magnets and webinars. Discuss how to make the offer irresistible, highlight the benefits, and create a sense of urgency.

i. Adapting Direct Response Copy for Different Audiences: Discuss how to adapt direct response copy for different target audiences. Touch on key considerations like language and tone, addressing specific pain points, and highlighting different benefits.

j. Direct Response Copy Mistakes to Avoid: Share common direct response copy mistakes that can turn readers off and prevent them from taking action. Discuss issues like not being benefit-driven enough, lack of specificity, and not using a clear call-to-action. Offer tips for avoiding these mistakes.

4. **Web Copywriting: Assisting with writing engaging and user-friendly web content, including homepage copy, product descriptions, and landing pages.**

   a. Writing Engaging Homepage Copy: Share your insights on how to create homepage copy that captures the attention of visitors and encourages them to explore the rest of the site. Discuss how to create a clear message, highlight the benefits, and include a strong call-to-action.

   b. Crafting Compelling Product Descriptions: Offer guidance on crafting product descriptions that not only describe the product but also highlight its unique benefits and features. Discuss how to use storytelling, create a sense of urgency, and make the product easy to visualize.

   c. Landing Page Copywriting: Describe the key elements of successful landing page copy, including creating a clear value proposition, making a strong offer, and including a clear call-to-action. Offer tips on using persuasive language and visuals to encourage visitors to take the desired action.

   d. Writing User-Friendly Web Copy: Discuss the importance of writing web copy that is easy to read and understand. Touch on key considerations like using simple language, breaking up long paragraphs, and making the copy scannable.

e. The Power of Visuals in Web Copy: Explain how to use visuals to enhance web copy and make it more engaging. Discuss the use of images, videos, and infographics, and offer tips on how to choose visuals that complement the copy.

f. Creating Compelling About Us Pages: Offer guidance on crafting about us pages that effectively communicate the company's story and values. Discuss how to create a compelling narrative, use language that resonates with the target audience, and highlight the company's unique features.

g. Writing for Mobile Devices: Describe the unique challenges and opportunities of writing for mobile devices and offer tips on how to create web copy that is optimized for mobile. Discuss how to make the copy scannable, using concise language, and making the call-to-action clear.

h. Creating Content for Blogs: Offer guidance on how to craft engaging and shareable blog content that resonates with the target audience. Discuss how to choose topics, use storytelling, and encourage engagement through comments and social sharing.

i. Copywriting for E-commerce Websites: Describe the key considerations for writing effective copy for e-commerce websites. Discuss how to create product descriptions that are benefit-driven, how to use persuasive language, and how to create a sense of urgency.

j. Web Copy Mistakes to Avoid: Share common web copy mistakes that can turn visitors off and prevent them from engaging with the content. Discuss issues like not focusing on benefits, not using clear calls-to-action, and not addressing objections. Offer tips for avoiding these mistakes.

5. **SEO Copywriting: Providing guidance on incorporating search engine optimization techniques into copywriting to improve content visibility and ranking on search engines.**

   a. Writing for SEO: Share your insights on how to write web copy that is optimized for search engines. Discuss how to use relevant keywords, create compelling headlines, and make the copy easy to read.

   b. Creating Content That Ranks: Offer guidance on how to create content that ranks well on search engines. Discuss how to use long-tail keywords, create content that answers common questions, and use internal and external links.

   c. Writing Meta Descriptions: Describe the importance of writing effective meta descriptions and offer tips on how to do so. Discuss how to include relevant keywords, use persuasive language, and make the description compelling.

d. Crafting Title Tags: Offer guidance on crafting effective title tags for web pages. Discuss how to use relevant keywords, create compelling headlines, and make the title tag unique and descriptive.

e. The Importance of User Intent: Explain the importance of understanding user intent when writing for SEO. Discuss how to create content that meets the needs of the target audience and provides value.

f. Writing for Local SEO: Describe the key considerations for writing web copy that is optimized for local search. Discuss how to use location-based keywords, include local references, and create content that is relevant to the local community.

g. Creating Content for Featured Snippets: Offer guidance on how to create content that is optimized for featured snippets. Discuss how to answer common questions, use concise language, and format the content in a way that makes it easy to read.

h. Writing for Voice Search: Describe the unique challenges and opportunities of writing web copy that is optimized for voice search. Discuss how to use conversational language, anticipate common queries, and provide clear and concise answers.

i. Using Schema Markup: Offer guidance on how to use schema markup to enhance SEO and make web content more visible to search engines. Discuss how to use schema for different types of content, such as products, reviews, and events.

j. SEO Copywriting Mistakes to Avoid: Share common SEO copywriting mistakes that can hurt a website's search engine ranking. Discuss issues like keyword stuffing, duplicate content, and not focusing on the target audience. Offer tips for avoiding these mistakes.

6. **Email Copywriting: Exploring best practices for crafting effective email copy that drives opens, clicks, and conversions.**

a. Writing Attention-Grabbing Subject Lines: Share your insights on how to write subject lines that capture the reader's attention and encourage them to open the email. Discuss how to use personalization, create a sense of urgency, and use curiosity to pique the reader's interest.

b. Crafting Compelling Email Copy: Offer guidance on crafting email copy that is engaging, persuasive, and relevant to the target audience. Discuss how to use storytelling, highlight benefits, and make a clear call-to-action.

c. Personalization in Email Copywriting: Describe the importance of personalizing email copy to increase engagement and drive conversions. Offer tips on how to use segmentation, data-driven personalization, and language that resonates with the recipient.

d. Creating Effective Email Templates: Discuss how to create email templates that are easy to customize and align with the brand's messaging. Offer tips on using visuals, including a clear call-to-action, and making the copy easy to scan.

e. A/B Testing Email Copy: Describe the importance of A/B testing in email copywriting and offer guidance on how to conduct effective tests. Discuss how to test different elements like subject lines, copy, and calls-to-action.

f. Email Copywriting for E-commerce: Offer guidance on how to craft email copy that effectively promotes products, increases conversions, and drives customer loyalty. Discuss how to use persuasive language, highlight benefits, and create a sense of urgency.

g. Writing Effective Welcome Emails: Describe the key elements of successful welcome emails and offer guidance on how to create them. Discuss how to use personalization, provide a clear value proposition, and create a sense of anticipation.

h. Writing Effective Cart Abandonment Emails: Discuss the importance of cart abandonment emails and offer tips on how to craft effective copy that encourages customers to complete the purchase. Discuss how to create a sense of urgency, highlight benefits, and include a clear call-to-action.

i. Email Copywriting Mistakes to Avoid: Share

common email copywriting mistakes that can hurt the effectiveness of email marketing campaigns. Discuss issues like not personalizing the email, using overly salesy language, and not making the copy easy to read. Offer tips for avoiding these mistakes.

j. The Power of Email Copywriting: Explain the importance of effective email copywriting in driving engagement, conversions, and customer loyalty. Discuss how to use storytelling, create a sense of urgency, and make the copy relevant to the recipient.

7. **Sales Letter Writing: Offering insights into writing persuasive sales letters that effectively communicate the value proposition and drive desired actions.**

a. Understanding Your Audience: Share your insights on how to understand your target audience and craft sales letters that resonate with them. Discuss how to use language and tone that aligns with their preferences, highlight benefits that matter to them, and address their pain points.

b. Crafting a Compelling Value Proposition: Offer guidance on how to create a value proposition that effectively communicates the unique benefits of the product or service. Discuss how to use storytelling, highlight features that set it apart from competitors, and use social proof to build credibility.

c. Writing Powerful Headlines: Describe the

importance of headlines in sales letters and offer tips on how to create headlines that capture the reader's attention and encourage them to read on. Discuss how to use benefit-driven language, create a sense of urgency, and use numbers and statistics to make the offer more compelling.

d. Using Persuasive Language: Discuss how to use persuasive language in sales letters to influence the reader's behavior. Offer tips on using emotional appeals, creating a sense of scarcity, and using language that creates a sense of exclusivity.

e. Making a Strong Call-to-Action: Describe the importance of a strong call-to-action in sales letters and offer guidance on how to create one. Discuss how to use clear and concise language, highlight the benefits of taking action, and create a sense of urgency.

f. Overcoming Objections: Offer guidance on how to address common objections in sales letters and provide solutions that alleviate concerns. Discuss how to use language that reassures the reader and builds trust, and highlight social proof that addresses objections.

g. Creating a Sense of Urgency: Describe the importance of creating a sense of urgency in sales letters and offer tips on how to do so. Discuss how to use language that creates a sense of scarcity, highlight time-limited offers, and use persuasive language that motivates the reader to take action.

h. Writing for Different Formats: Discuss how to adapt sales letters for different formats, such as email, landing pages, and direct mail. Touch on key considerations like headline length, visual elements, and call-to-action placement.

i. The Power of Storytelling: Explain the importance of storytelling in sales letters and offer guidance on how to use it effectively. Discuss how to create a narrative that engages the reader, highlights benefits, and creates an emotional connection.

j. Sales Letter Mistakes to Avoid: Share common sales letter mistakes that can hurt the effectiveness of the copy. Discuss issues like using generic language, not highlighting benefits, and not addressing objections. Offer tips for avoiding these mistakes.

8. **Copywriting Formulas: Discussing popular copywriting formulas, such as AIDA (Attention, Interest, Desire, Action) and PAS (Problem, Agitate, Solve), to guide content creation.**

a. Introduction to Copywriting Formulas: Provide an overview of popular copywriting formulas like AIDA, PAS, and FAB, and discuss their key components. Explain how they can be used to guide content creation and improve the effectiveness of copy.

b. AIDA Formula: Describe the AIDA formula (Attention, Interest, Desire, Action) and offer guidance on how to use it effectively. Discuss how to create headlines that capture attention, build interest, create desire, and make a clear call-to-action.

c. PAS Formula: Offer guidance on how to use the PAS formula (Problem, Agitate, Solve) to address the reader's pain points and offer a solution. Discuss how to identify the reader's problem, use language that creates urgency, and offer a solution that addresses their concerns.

d. FAB Formula: Discuss the FAB formula (Features, Advantages, Benefits) and offer guidance on how to use it effectively. Discuss how to highlight product features, explain how they provide advantages, and use language that highlights the benefits to the reader.

e. The Power of Emotional Appeals: Explain the importance of emotional appeals in copywriting and offer guidance on how to use them effectively. Discuss how to use language that creates an emotional connection with the reader, highlights the benefits that matter to them, and addresses their pain points.

f. The Problem-Solution Formula: Describe the problem-solution formula and offer guidance on how to use it effectively. Discuss how to identify the reader's problem, create a sense of urgency, and offer a solution that addresses their concerns.

g. The Testimonial Formula: Discuss the importance of social proof in copywriting and offer guidance on how to use the testimonial formula effectively. Discuss how to choose the right testimonials, highlight key benefits, and use language that emphasizes the credibility of the source.

h. The Guarantee Formula: Offer guidance on how to use guarantees effectively in copywriting. Discuss how to create a strong guarantee that addresses the reader's concerns and creates a sense of trust.

i. The Comparison Formula: Describe the comparison formula and offer guidance on how to use it effectively. Discuss how to compare the product or service to competitors, highlight key benefits, and use language that emphasizes the superiority of the product or service.

j. Copywriting Formulas Mistakes to Avoid: Share common mistakes in using copywriting formulas that can hurt the effectiveness of the copy. Discuss issues like using formulas too rigidly, not adapting to the target audience, and not being creative enough. Offer tips for avoiding these mistakes.

9. **Copy Editing and Proofreading: Providing advice on editing and proofreading copy to ensure clarity, accuracy, and consistency.**

a. The Importance of Editing and Proofreading: Explain the importance of editing and proofreading copy to ensure clarity, accuracy, and consistency. Discuss how it improves the effectiveness of the copy and avoids misunderstandings or errors.

b. Understanding the Target Audience: Discuss how understanding the target audience can guide the editing and proofreading process. Touch on key considerations like language, tone, and terminology.

c. Grammar and Spelling: Offer guidance on correcting grammar and spelling errors in copy. Discuss common mistakes like subject-verb agreement, misplaced modifiers, and homophones, and provide tips for avoiding them.

d. Punctuation and Capitalization: Describe the importance of proper punctuation and capitalization in copy and offer guidance on how to use them effectively. Discuss common mistakes like missing or misused punctuation marks, and provide tips for avoiding them.

e. Formatting and Consistency: Discuss how formatting and consistency affect the readability and professionalism of copy. Offer tips on creating a consistent style, using headings and subheadings effectively, and using bullet points and lists.

f. Content Accuracy: Discuss how to ensure the accuracy of facts, statistics, and other information included in the copy. Touch on key considerations like using reliable sources, fact-checking, and citing sources when necessary.

g. Eliminating Jargon: Discuss the importance of eliminating jargon and technical language that may confuse or alienate the reader. Offer tips on using plain language, avoiding industry-specific terminology, and providing context when necessary.

h. Adapting to Different Formats: Discuss how editing and proofreading may differ depending on the format of the copy, such as web copy, email, or print materials. Touch on key considerations like formatting, headlines, and calls-to-action.

i. Collaborating with the Author: Offer guidance on how to collaborate effectively with the author during the editing and proofreading process. Discuss how to provide feedback that is constructive, respectful, and actionable.

j. Editing and Proofreading Mistakes to Avoid: Share common mistakes in editing and proofreading that can hurt the effectiveness of the copy. Discuss issues like not proofreading carefully enough, not using style guides effectively, and not addressing the target audience's needs. Offer tips for avoiding these mistakes.

10. **Copywriting for Different Industries: Exploring the nuances of writing copy for specific industries, such as healthcare, technology, or finance, and adapting messaging to cater to the target audience.**

a. Healthcare Industry: Offer guidance on writing copy for the healthcare industry, including key considerations like patient empathy, accuracy of medical information, and clear communication of complex medical concepts.

b. Technology Industry: Discuss how to write copy that effectively communicates technical concepts and features to a non-technical audience. Touch on key considerations like highlighting benefits, avoiding jargon, and using visual aids.

c. Finance Industry: Offer guidance on writing copy for the finance industry, including key considerations like building trust, emphasizing benefits, and creating a sense of urgency. Discuss how to use language that is clear, concise, and easy to understand.

d. Retail Industry: Discuss how to write copy that effectively communicates the value proposition of products or services in the retail industry. Touch on key considerations like highlighting benefits, creating a sense of urgency, and using persuasive language.

e. Hospitality Industry: Offer guidance on writing copy for the hospitality industry, including key considerations like creating an emotional connection with the reader, highlighting unique features and benefits, and using language that creates a sense of exclusivity.

f. Education Industry: Discuss how to write copy

that effectively communicates the value proposition of educational products or services. Touch on key considerations like highlighting benefits, addressing the reader's pain points, and creating a sense of urgency.

g. Nonprofit Industry: Offer guidance on writing copy for the nonprofit industry, including key considerations like building empathy, highlighting the impact of donations, and creating a sense of urgency. Discuss how to use language that is clear, concise, and easy to understand.

h. Automotive Industry: Discuss how to write copy that effectively communicates the value proposition of automotive products or services. Touch on key considerations like highlighting benefits, addressing the reader's pain points, and creating a sense of urgency.

i. Beauty Industry: Offer guidance on writing copy for the beauty industry, including key considerations like creating an emotional connection with the reader, highlighting unique features and benefits, and using persuasive language. Discuss how to use language that is clear, concise, and easy to understand.

j. Real Estate Industry: Discuss how to write copy that effectively communicates the value proposition of real estate products or services. Touch on key considerations like highlighting benefits, addressing the reader's pain points, and creating a sense of urgency.

4

Creative Writing Prompts

1. **Fiction Writing: Offering guidance on crafting engaging stories, including character development, plot structure, and narrative techniques.**
   a. Developing Compelling Characters: Offer guidance on developing compelling characters in fiction writing, including key considerations like backstory, motivation, and character flaws. Discuss how to use character development to drive the plot and engage the reader.
   b. Plot Structure: Discuss the importance of plot structure in fiction writing and offer guidance on creating a compelling story arc. Touch on key considerations like the inciting incident, rising action, climax, and resolution.
   c. Point of View: Offer guidance on choosing the right point of view for a story and using it effectively. Discuss the differences between first-

person, second-person, and third-person point of view and how to use each to create a compelling story.

d. Dialogue: Discuss the importance of dialogue in fiction writing and offer guidance on writing realistic and engaging dialogue. Touch on key considerations like using dialogue to reveal character, advancing the plot, and creating tension.

e. Setting: Offer guidance on using setting effectively in fiction writing. Discuss how to use description to create a sense of place, setting as a reflection of character, and setting as a catalyst for conflict.

f. Narrative Techniques: Discuss how to use narrative techniques like foreshadowing, flashback, and symbolism to create a compelling story. Touch on key considerations like using these techniques to create tension, reveal character, and advance the plot.

g. Voice and Tone: Offer guidance on developing a unique voice and tone in fiction writing. Discuss how to use language and sentence structure to create a unique style that engages the reader and reflects the story.

h. Writing Style: Discuss the importance of writing style in fiction writing and offer guidance on how to develop a style that suits the story and engages the reader. Touch on key considerations like tone, pacing, and the use of literary devices.

i. Editing and Revising: Offer guidance on the editing and revision process in fiction writing. Discuss how to identify and address weak points in the story, how to refine the language and style, and how to make the story more engaging for the reader.

j. Critique and Feedback: Discuss the importance of critique and feedback in fiction writing and offer guidance on how to give and receive feedback constructively. Touch on key considerations like setting boundaries, being respectful, and using feedback to improve the story.

2. **Poetry: Assisting with the writing and analysis of various poetic forms, such as sonnets, haikus, and free verse, as well as exploring poetic devices and themes.**

   a. Understanding Poetic Form: Offer guidance on understanding the different poetic forms, such as sonnets, haikus, and free verse. Discuss the structure and conventions of each form and how to use them to create a compelling poem.

   b. Poetic Devices: Discuss the different poetic devices, such as metaphor, simile, and alliteration, and how to use them effectively in poetry. Touch on key considerations like using devices to create meaning, evoke emotion, and enhance the imagery of the poem.

   c. Theme and Imagery: Offer guidance on developing themes and imagery in poetry. Discuss how to use language and imagery to create a sense of meaning and emotional resonance in the poem.

d. Voice and Tone: Discuss the importance of voice and tone in poetry and offer guidance on developing a unique style that engages the reader. Touch on key considerations like using language and sentence structure to create a unique style that reflects the poem.

e. Poetic Meter: Offer guidance on understanding poetic meter and using it effectively in poetry. Discuss the different types of meter, such as iambic pentameter and trochaic tetrameter, and how to use them to create rhythm and pacing in the poem.

f. Form and Structure: Discuss the importance of form and structure in poetry and offer guidance on choosing the right form for the poem. Touch on key considerations like using form to enhance meaning, create contrast, and evoke emotion.

g. Revision and Editing: Offer guidance on the revision and editing process in poetry. Discuss how to refine language and imagery, how to address weak points in the poem, and how to make the poem more engaging for the reader.

h. Performance and Reading: Discuss the importance of performance and reading in poetry and offer guidance on how to prepare and deliver a powerful reading of a poem. Touch on key considerations like voice, pacing, and the use of gestures.

i. Poetry Critique and Feedback: Discuss the importance of critique and feedback in poetry and offer guidance on how to give and receive feedback constructively. Touch on key considerations like setting boundaries, being respectful, and using feedback to improve the poem.

j. Exploring Poetic Themes: Offer guidance on exploring different poetic themes, such as love, nature, and politics. Discuss how to use language and imagery to explore these themes in a meaningful and engaging way.

3. **Creative Nonfiction: Discussing the art of writing creative nonfiction, which combines factual storytelling with narrative and stylistic techniques typically found in fiction.**

a. Finding Your Narrative Voice: Offer guidance on finding and developing a unique voice in creative nonfiction writing. Discuss how to use language, tone, and style to create a distinctive narrative voice that engages the reader.

b. The Art of Research: Discuss the importance of research in creative nonfiction writing and offer guidance on how to conduct effective research. Touch on key considerations like finding reliable sources, managing information, and integrating research into the narrative.

c. Narrative and Structure: Offer guidance on

developing a compelling narrative and structure in creative nonfiction writing. Discuss how to use narrative techniques like scene-setting, characterization, and dialogue to engage the reader and create a cohesive story.

d. Balancing Fact and Fiction: Discuss the delicate balance between fact and fiction in creative nonfiction writing and offer guidance on how to use narrative techniques typically found in fiction to enhance the story while maintaining accuracy and integrity.

e. Writing Memoir: Offer guidance on writing memoir in creative nonfiction, including key considerations like memory, reflection, and perspective. Discuss how to use personal experience to engage the reader and create a compelling narrative.

f. Writing Personal Essays: Discuss the art of writing personal essays in creative nonfiction, including key considerations like voice, structure, and theme. Offer guidance on how to use personal experience to explore universal themes and create a relatable story.

g. Writing Travel Writing: Offer guidance on writing travel writing in creative nonfiction, including key considerations like voice, structure, and sensory detail. Discuss how to use personal experience to engage the reader and create a vivid portrayal of a place.

   h. Editing and Revision: Offer guidance on the editing and revision process in creative nonfiction writing. Discuss how to refine language and style, address weak points in the narrative, and make the story more engaging for the reader.

   i. Critique and Feedback: Discuss the importance of critique and feedback in creative nonfiction writing and offer guidance on how to give and receive feedback constructively. Touch on key considerations like setting boundaries, being respectful, and using feedback to improve the story.

   j. Publishing Creative Nonfiction: Offer guidance on the publishing process for creative nonfiction, including finding agents and publishers, writing query letters, and submitting work for publication.

4. **Screenwriting: Providing insights into the process of writing scripts for film, television, or theater, including formatting, dialogue, and story structure.**

   a. Script Formatting: Offer guidance on script formatting for film, television, or theater. Discuss industry-standard formatting, including elements like sluglines, action blocks, and dialogue.

   b. Character Development: Discuss the importance of character development in screenwriting and offer guidance on creating compelling and well-rounded characters. Touch on key considerations like backstory, motivation, and character flaws.

   c. Writing Dialogue: Offer guidance on writing

effective dialogue in screenwriting, including key considerations like voice, subtext, and pacing. Discuss how to use dialogue to reveal character, advance the plot, and create tension.

d. Story Structure: Discuss the importance of story structure in screenwriting and offer guidance on creating a compelling story arc. Touch on key considerations like the inciting incident, rising action, climax, and resolution.

e. Visual Storytelling: Offer guidance on using visual storytelling to enhance the story in screenwriting. Discuss how to use visual elements like camera angles, lighting, and mise-en-scene to create meaning and emotion in a scene.

f. Writing Treatments: Discuss the importance of writing treatments in screenwriting and offer guidance on how to write a compelling treatment that sells the story.

g. Pitching and Selling: Offer guidance on the pitching and selling process in screenwriting, including how to write a logline, create a pitch deck, and approach agents and producers.

h. Collaboration and Feedback: Discuss the importance of collaboration and feedback in screenwriting and offer guidance on how to work effectively with co-writers, directors, and producers.

i. Writing for Different Mediums: Offer guidance on writing for different mediums, such as film, television, and theater. Discuss key differences in formatting, structure, and storytelling, and offer tips for adapting the story to the medium.

j. Genre and Tone: Offer guidance on developing genre and tone in screenwriting. Discuss how to use genre conventions and tone to create meaning, evoke emotion, and engage the audience.

5. **Flash Fiction and Short Stories: Exploring the craft of writing short fiction, including the unique challenges and techniques for creating impactful stories within a limited word count.**

a. Flash Fiction vs. Short Stories: Offer guidance on the difference between flash fiction and short stories and how to write both effectively. Touch on key considerations like length, structure, and narrative techniques.

b. Narrative Techniques: Discuss the different narrative techniques used in flash fiction and short stories, such as characterization, dialogue, and setting. Offer guidance on how to use these techniques effectively to engage the reader and create a compelling story.

c. Writing with Constraints: Offer guidance on writing flash fiction and short stories with constraints, such as limited word count or a specific theme. Discuss how to use constraints to enhance creativity and craft a compelling story.

d. Developing Plot: Discuss the importance of plot in flash fiction and short stories and offer guidance on developing a compelling plot within a limited word count. Touch on key considerations like pacing, conflict, and resolution.

e. Character Development: Offer guidance on developing characters in flash fiction and short stories, including key considerations like backstory, motivation, and character flaws. Discuss how to use characterization to engage the reader and create a relatable story.

f. Setting and Description: Offer guidance on using setting and description effectively in flash fiction and short stories. Discuss how to create a vivid and immersive world within a limited word count.

g. Writing Endings: Discuss the importance of endings in flash fiction and short stories and offer guidance on writing satisfying and impactful endings. Touch on key considerations like resolution, closure, and leaving the reader with a lasting impression.

h. Writing Dialogue: Offer guidance on writing effective dialogue in flash fiction and short stories. Discuss how to use dialogue to reveal character, advance the plot, and create tension within a limited word count.

i. Editing and Revising: Offer guidance on the editing and revising process in flash fiction and short stories. Discuss how to refine language and style, address weak points in the narrative, and make the story more engaging for the reader.

    j. Submitting and Publishing: Offer guidance on submitting and publishing flash fiction and short stories, including finding markets, writing cover letters, and submitting work for publication.

6. **Memoir and Personal Essays: Offering guidance on writing memoirs and personal essays, which focus on sharing personal experiences, reflections, and insights.**

    a. Finding Your Story: Offer guidance on finding and developing a personal story to share in memoirs and personal essays. Discuss how to identify key experiences and insights, and use them to create a compelling narrative.

    b. Narrative and Structure: Offer guidance on developing a compelling narrative and structure in memoirs and personal essays. Discuss how to use narrative techniques like scene-setting, characterization, and dialogue to engage the reader and create a cohesive story.

    c. Voice and Tone: Discuss the importance of voice and tone in memoirs and personal essays, and offer guidance on finding a unique and authentic voice. Touch on key considerations like language, style, and point of view.

    d. Writing Style and Techniques: Offer guidance on using writing style and techniques to enhance the impact of memoirs and personal essays. Discuss how to use elements like metaphor, symbolism, and imagery to create meaning and emotion in the story.

e. Reflection and Insight: Discuss the importance of reflection and insight in memoirs and personal essays, and offer guidance on how to use personal experience to explore universal themes and create a relatable story.

f. Writing About Trauma: Offer guidance on writing about traumatic experiences in memoirs and personal essays, including key considerations like self-care, sensitivity, and responsible representation.

g. Editing and Revision: Offer guidance on the editing and revision process in memoirs and personal essays. Discuss how to refine language and style, address weak points in the narrative, and make the story more engaging for the reader.

h. Critique and Feedback: Discuss the importance of critique and feedback in memoirs and personal essays, and offer guidance on how to give and receive feedback constructively. Touch on key considerations like setting boundaries, being respectful, and using feedback to improve the story.

i. Publishing Memoirs and Personal Essays: Offer guidance on the publishing process for memoirs and personal essays, including finding agents and publishers, writing query letters, and submitting work for publication.

   j. Finding Your Audience: Discuss the importance of finding the right audience for memoirs and personal essays, and offer guidance on how to identify and reach that audience through marketing and promotion.

7. **Worldbuilding: Assisting with the creation of vivid, immersive settings and worlds for stories, including cultural, geographic, and historical elements.**

   a. Developing Culture: Offer guidance on developing cultures and societies in worldbuilding. Discuss key considerations like history, religion, and social structures, and offer tips for creating immersive and believable cultures.

   b. Creating Geography: Discuss the importance of geography in worldbuilding, and offer guidance on creating realistic and interesting landscapes, environments, and ecosystems.

   c. Historical Context: Offer guidance on incorporating historical context into worldbuilding, including key considerations like technology, politics, and art.

   d. Magic and Fantasy: Discuss the use of magic and fantasy elements in worldbuilding, and offer guidance on how to use them effectively to enhance the story and create meaning.

   e. Language and Communication: Offer guidance on developing languages and communication systems in worldbuilding, and discuss how to use them to enhance the story and create immersion.

f. Creature and Character Design: Offer guidance on designing creatures and characters in worldbuilding, including key considerations like biology, behavior, and culture.

g. Conflict and Politics: Discuss the importance of conflict and politics in worldbuilding, and offer guidance on how to create engaging and realistic conflicts and political systems.

h. Writing Style and Techniques: Offer guidance on using writing style and techniques to enhance the impact of worldbuilding. Discuss how to use elements like metaphor, symbolism, and imagery to create meaning and emotion in the story.

i. Editing and Revision: Offer guidance on the editing and revision process in worldbuilding. Discuss how to refine language and style, address weak points in the narrative, and make the world more engaging for the reader.

j. Incorporating Feedback: Discuss the importance of incorporating feedback in worldbuilding, and offer guidance on how to incorporate feedback from beta readers, editors, and other sources to improve the worldbuilding and make it more compelling for the reader.

8. **Dialogue and Voice: Providing advice on crafting authentic and engaging dialogue, as well as developing distinct character voices and narrative perspectives.**

a. Developing Voice: Offer guidance on developing

a distinct voice for characters and narratives. Discuss key considerations like tone, language, and point of view, and offer tips for creating unique and memorable voices.

b. Crafting Dialogue: Discuss the art of crafting dialogue, including how to make it sound natural, reveal character, and advance the plot. Offer guidance on using dialogue effectively to engage the reader and create tension.

c. Characterization Through Dialogue: Discuss how to use dialogue to reveal character traits, motivations, and conflicts. Offer guidance on creating dynamic and memorable characters through dialogue.

d. Writing Believable Dialogue: Offer guidance on writing dialogue that feels authentic and believable, including tips for incorporating regionalisms, slang, and accents.

e. Subtext in Dialogue: Discuss the use of subtext in dialogue, and offer guidance on how to use it effectively to create tension and add depth to the story.

f. Writing Inner Dialogue: Offer guidance on writing inner dialogue, including how to use it to reveal character thoughts, emotions, and conflicts.

g. Dialogue Tags and Beats: Discuss the use of dialogue tags and beats, and offer guidance on how to use them to create clarity, pacing, and tension.

h. Point of View and Dialogue: Offer guidance on

how to use point of view to enhance the impact of dialogue, and how to switch between different points of view effectively.

i. Writing Memorable Lines: Discuss the importance of memorable lines in dialogue, and offer guidance on how to craft lines that stick with the reader.

j. Revising Dialogue: Offer guidance on the revision process for dialogue, including how to refine language, address weak points in the narrative, and make the dialogue more engaging for the reader.

9. **Genre Writing: Discussing the conventions and techniques associated with specific creative writing genres, such as mystery, romance, science fiction, or fantasy.**

a. Writing Mystery: Discuss the conventions and techniques associated with writing mystery, including creating suspense, developing red herrings, and revealing clues.

b. Writing Romance: Offer guidance on writing romance, including how to create compelling characters, develop romantic tension, and write satisfying endings.

c. Writing Science Fiction: Discuss the conventions and techniques associated with writing science fiction, including worldbuilding, creating futuristic technologies, and exploring social issues.

d. Writing Fantasy: Offer guidance on writing

fantasy, including how to create compelling magical systems, develop richly imagined worlds, and write epic battles.

e. Writing Horror: Discuss the conventions and techniques associated with writing horror, including creating fear and tension, developing terrifying creatures or scenarios, and using setting and tone to create mood.

f. Writing Historical Fiction: Offer guidance on writing historical fiction, including researching and recreating historical settings and characters, and using imagination to fill in gaps in the historical record.

g. Writing Thriller: Discuss the conventions and techniques associated with writing thrillers, including creating high stakes, developing plot twists, and using pacing to keep readers engaged.

h. Writing Young Adult Fiction: Offer guidance on writing young adult fiction, including developing compelling teenage characters, addressing relevant social issues, and balancing adult themes with age-appropriate content.

i. Writing Comedy: Discuss the conventions and techniques associated with writing comedy, including using humor to reveal character, developing comedic timing, and balancing humor with plot and theme.

j. Writing Drama: Offer guidance on writing drama, including developing compelling characters with complex motivations, using conflict to drive the story, and exploring themes related to identity, relationships, and social issues.

10. **Writing Prompts and Exercises: Offering creative writing prompts and exercises to help spark inspiration, overcome writer's block, and hone writing skills.**

   a. Character Development: Offer a writing prompt that challenges writers to develop a compelling character, including backstory, motivation, and personality traits.

   b. Setting Development: Offer a writing prompt that challenges writers to develop a compelling setting, including sensory details, historical context, and cultural elements.

   c. Dialogue Practice: Offer a writing exercise that challenges writers to practice writing effective dialogue, including creating a dialogue-driven scene or conversation.

   d. Plot Development: Offer a writing prompt that challenges writers to develop a compelling plot, including identifying conflict, building tension, and creating plot twists.

   e. Image-Based Prompts: Offer a writing prompt that uses images as inspiration for a piece of creative writing, including visual prompts like photographs or artwork.

   f. Flash Fiction: Offer a writing prompt that challenges writers to write a complete story within a limited word count, typically 500-1000 words.

g. Stream of Consciousness: Offer a writing exercise that challenges writers to write a stream of consciousness piece, without worrying about plot or structure.

h. Genre Mash-Up: Offer a writing prompt that challenges writers to combine two different genres in their writing, creating a hybrid genre.

i. Time-Based Prompts: Offer a writing prompt that challenges writers to write within a specific time frame, such as 15 minutes or an hour.

j. Reverse Perspective: Offer a writing prompt that challenges writers to write a scene from the perspective of a secondary character or a different point of view.

5

E-Commerce Prompts

1. **E-Commerce Platforms: Offering guidance on selecting and using various e-commerce platforms, such as Shopify, WooCommerce, and Magento.**
   a. [E-Commerce Platform Comparison]: Provide a comparison of popular e-commerce platforms, such as Shopify, WooCommerce, and Magento, including their features, pricing, and target audience.
   b. [Selecting the Right E-Commerce Platform]: Discuss key factors to consider when selecting an e-commerce platform for an online store, including scalability, ease of use, and customization options.
   c. [E-Commerce Platform Migration]: Offer guidance on migrating an existing online store from one e-commerce platform to another, including potential challenges and best practices.

d. [E-Commerce Platform Integrations]: Examine the availability and importance of integrations with third-party tools and services, such as payment gateways, marketing apps, and inventory management systems, for various e-commerce platforms.

e. [Customizing E-Commerce Platforms]: Discuss customization options for popular e-commerce platforms, including themes, plugins, and custom code, to tailor the store to specific business needs.

f. [Optimizing E-Commerce Platform Performance]: Share tips and best practices for optimizing e-commerce platform performance, such as site speed, mobile-friendliness, and search engine optimization (SEO).

g. [E-Commerce Platform Security]: Examine security features and best practices for various e-commerce platforms, including SSL certificates, PCI compliance, and data protection measures.

h. [E-Commerce Platform Support]: Discuss the availability and quality of customer support for popular e-commerce platforms, including self-help resources, live support, and community forums.

i. [E-Commerce Platform Case Studies]: Share case studies of successful online stores built on different e-commerce platforms, highlighting their features, growth strategies, and lessons learned.

    j. [E-Commerce Platform Trends]: Examine emerging trends and innovations in e-commerce platforms, such as headless commerce, AI-powered personalization, and omnichannel integration.

2. **Online Store Design and User Experience: Providing advice on designing and optimizing online stores for user experience, conversion, and accessibility.**

    a. [Design Principles for Online Stores]: Discuss fundamental design principles for creating an effective and visually appealing online store, such as color theory, typography, and layout.

    b. [User Experience (UX) Best Practices]: Share best practices for optimizing user experience on e-commerce websites, including navigation, search functionality, and page load times.

    c. [Conversion Rate Optimization]: Offer guidance on implementing conversion rate optimization strategies for online stores, such as A/B testing, calls-to-action, and trust signals.

    d. [Mobile-First E-Commerce Design]: Discuss the importance of mobile-first design for e-commerce websites and provide tips for creating a seamless and responsive mobile shopping experience.

    e. [Accessibility in E-Commerce]: Examine the importance of accessibility in online store design and share tips for making e-commerce websites accessible to all users, including those with disabilities.

    f. [Product Page Optimization]: Provide advice on

optimizing product pages for increased conversions, including product photography, descriptions, and customer reviews.

g. [E-Commerce Site Structure]: Discuss best practices for structuring an e-commerce website for optimal user experience and search engine performance, including category organization and URL structure.

h. [E-Commerce Website Redesign]: Offer guidance on approaching an e-commerce website redesign project, including identifying areas for improvement, planning, and implementation.

i. [User Testing for E-Commerce]: Examine the role of user testing in optimizing online store design and user experience, including methods for gathering feedback and implementing changes.

j. [E-Commerce Design Trends]: Explore emerging trends and innovations in e-commerce website design, such as 3D product visualization, augmented reality, and interactive content.

3. **Product Sourcing and Inventory Management: Discussing strategies for sourcing products and managing inventory in an e-commerce business.**

    a. [Product Sourcing Strategies]: Discuss various strategies for sourcing products for an e-commerce business, including dropshipping, wholesale purchasing, and private labeling.

    b. [Supplier Selection]: Provide guidance on selecting and vetting suppliers for e-commerce businesses, including considerations such as reliability, product quality, and communication.

c. [Inventory Management Techniques]: Share best practices for managing inventory in an e-commerce business, including stock forecasting, reorder points, and safety stock calculations.

d. [Managing Stock Levels]: Discuss strategies for effectively managing stock levels in an e-commerce business, including techniques for preventing stockouts and overstock situations.

e. [Warehouse and Storage Solutions]: Explore various warehouse and storage solutions for e-commerce businesses, including self-storage, third-party logistics (3PL), and on-demand warehousing.

f. [Inventory Management Software]: Provide an overview of popular inventory management software solutions for e-commerce businesses, including their features, pricing, and integration capabilities.

g. [Product Sourcing Challenges]: Examine common challenges in product sourcing and inventory management for e-commerce businesses, along with strategies for overcoming these obstacles.

h. [Sustainable Product Sourcing]: Discuss the importance of sustainable and ethical product sourcing practices in e-commerce and share tips for implementing such practices.

   i. [Managing Returns and Excess Inventory]: Offer guidance on managing returns and excess inventory in an e-commerce business, including restocking, liquidation, and donation options.

   j. [Inventory Management Metrics]: Share key inventory management metrics for e-commerce businesses, such as inventory turnover, sell-through rate, and days of inventory on hand.

4. **Payment Processing and Security: Providing information on selecting and implementing secure payment processing solutions for online stores.**

   a. [Choosing a Payment Gateway]: Provide guidance on selecting the right payment gateway for an e-commerce business, considering factors such as fees, accepted payment methods, and ease of integration.

   b. [Secure Payment Processing]: Discuss the importance of secure payment processing in e-commerce and share tips for ensuring transaction security, such as SSL encryption and PCI compliance.

   c. [Fraud Prevention in E-Commerce]: Examine common types of e-commerce fraud and offer strategies for preventing and detecting fraudulent transactions.

   d. [Multi-Currency Payment Processing]: Explore options and best practices for accepting and processing payments in multiple currencies for international e-commerce businesses.

e. [Alternative Payment Methods]: Discuss the role of alternative payment methods, such as digital wallets and cryptocurrencies, in e-commerce and their potential impact on customer experience and conversion rates.

f. [Managing Payment Disputes]: Offer guidance on handling payment disputes and chargebacks in e-commerce, including prevention strategies and dispute resolution processes.

g. [Payment Processing Regulations]: Examine relevant regulations and industry standards for payment processing in e-commerce, such as PCI DSS, GDPR, and PSD2.

h. [Recurring Billing and Subscriptions]: Provide advice on implementing recurring billing and subscription-based payment models in e-commerce, including payment gateway considerations and customer experience tips.

i. [Mobile Payment Optimization]: Discuss strategies for optimizing mobile payment experiences in e-commerce, such as responsive design, mobile wallets, and one-click checkout options.

j. [Payment Processing Trends]: Explore emerging trends and innovations in e-commerce payment processing, such as biometric authentication, instant payments, and voice commerce.

5. **Shipping and Fulfillment: Offering guidance on setting up and managing shipping and fulfillment processes for e-commerce businesses.**

a. [Shipping Strategy Basics]: Discuss the fundamentals of creating a shipping strategy for an e-commerce business, including shipping methods, pricing, and delivery speed.

b. [Selecting a Shipping Carrier]: Provide guidance on selecting the right shipping carrier for an e-commerce business, considering factors such as costs, service levels, and geographical coverage.

c. [Packaging and Branding]: Share tips for creating effective and branded packaging for e-commerce shipments, including material selection, design, and sustainability considerations.

d. [Fulfillment Options]: Examine various fulfillment options for e-commerce businesses, such as in-house fulfillment, third-party logistics (3PL), and fulfillment by Amazon (FBA).

e. [International Shipping]: Discuss strategies and considerations for managing international shipping in e-commerce, including customs, taxes, and regulatory compliance.

f. [Shipping Automation]: Explore shipping automation tools and software solutions for e-commerce businesses, including their features, benefits, and integration capabilities.

g. [Returns and Reverse Logistics]: Offer guidance on managing returns and reverse logistics in an e-commerce business, including return policies, processes, and customer communication.

h. [Tracking and Customer Communication]:

Share best practices for providing shipment tracking information and proactive communication to customers during the shipping process.

i. [Shipping Cost Optimization]: Discuss strategies for optimizing shipping costs in e-commerce, such as negotiated rates, carrier discounts, and dimensional weight pricing.

j. [Shipping and Fulfillment Trends]: Examine emerging trends and innovations in e-commerce shipping and fulfillment, such as drone deliveries, on-demand warehousing, and smart packaging.

6. **E-Commerce Marketing: Discussing various marketing strategies and tactics for promoting and growing an e-commerce business.**

a. [E-Commerce Marketing Strategies]: Provide an overview of effective marketing strategies for e-commerce businesses, including content marketing, social media, and email marketing.

b. [Search Engine Optimization (SEO)]: Discuss best practices for optimizing e-commerce websites for search engines, including on-page, off-page, and technical SEO tactics.

c. [Social Media Marketing]: Examine the role of social media marketing in e-commerce, including platform selection, content creation, and advertising strategies.

d. [Email Marketing for E-Commerce]: Share tips for creating effective email marketing campaigns for e-commerce businesses, including list building, segmentation, and automation.

e. [Influencer Marketing]: Discuss the potential benefits and challenges of influencer marketing for e-commerce businesses, including collaboration strategies and measuring ROI.

f. [Paid Advertising]: Provide guidance on implementing paid advertising campaigns for e-commerce businesses, including search engine marketing (SEM) and social media advertising.

g. [Promotions and Discounts]: Offer strategies for creating and managing promotions and discounts in e-commerce, such as seasonal sales, flash sales, and customer loyalty programs.

h. [E-Commerce Content Marketing]: Explore the role of content marketing in e-commerce, including blog posts, product guides, and video content, to drive traffic and conversions.

i. [Conversion Rate Optimization (CRO)]: Discuss techniques for optimizing conversion rates on e-commerce websites, including site design, messaging, and user experience improvements.

j. [E-Commerce Marketing Analytics]: Share insights into tracking and analyzing e-commerce marketing performance using analytics tools and data-driven decision-making.

7. **Customer Service and Support: Providing advice on handling customer service and support for online**

businesses, including returns, refunds, and dispute resolution.

a. [Customer Service Basics]: Discuss the fundamentals of providing exceptional customer service and support for e-commerce businesses, including communication channels, response times, and issue resolution.

b. [Live Chat and Chatbots]: Examine the role of live chat and chatbots in e-commerce customer service, including their benefits, limitations, and implementation considerations.

c. [Social Media Customer Service]: Explore the importance of providing customer service through social media platforms and share tips for managing and monitoring social media inquiries.

d. [E-Commerce Returns and Refunds]: Offer guidance on creating and managing return and refund policies for e-commerce businesses, balancing customer satisfaction with business profitability.

e. [Managing Negative Reviews]: Discuss strategies for effectively addressing and managing negative customer reviews on e-commerce platforms and review sites.

f. [Customer Support Software]: Provide an overview of popular customer support software solutions for e-commerce businesses, including their features, pricing, and integration capabilities.

g. [Building Customer Loyalty]: Share strategies

for building customer loyalty and fostering repeat business in e-commerce, such as loyalty programs, personalized experiences, and exclusive offers.

h. [Dispute Resolution]: Offer guidance on handling customer disputes and resolving issues effectively to maintain customer satisfaction and protect your e-commerce business reputation.

i. [Customer Service Outsourcing]: Explore the pros and cons of outsourcing customer service for e-commerce businesses, including cost considerations, quality control, and scalability.

j. [Customer Service Metrics]: Discuss key customer service metrics for e-commerce businesses, such as first response time, customer satisfaction score, and resolution rate.

8. **Sales Tax and Compliance: Offering guidance on navigating sales tax and compliance issues for e-commerce businesses operating in multiple jurisdictions.**

a. [E-Commerce Sales Tax Basics]: Provide an overview of sales tax basics for e-commerce businesses, including nexus, tax rates, and exemptions.

b. [Sales Tax Compliance]: Discuss strategies for ensuring sales tax compliance in e-commerce businesses, including tax calculation, collection, and remittance processes.

c. [Multi-State Sales Tax]: Examine the challenges and considerations of managing sales tax compliance for e-commerce businesses operating in multiple states or jurisdictions.

d. [International Sales Tax]: Offer guidance on navigating sales tax and value-added tax (VAT) issues for e-commerce businesses selling products to customers in different countries.

e. [Tax-Exempt Sales]: Share strategies for identifying and managing tax-exempt sales in e-commerce, including documentation, verification, and reporting requirements.

f. [Sales Tax Software]: Explore sales tax software solutions for e-commerce businesses, including their features, pricing, and integration capabilities.

g. [E-Commerce Regulations]: Discuss relevant e-commerce regulations and industry standards, such as GDPR, CCPA, and ADA compliance, and their impact on e-commerce businesses.

h. [Audits and Penalties]: Provide advice on preparing for and managing sales tax audits and avoiding penalties for non-compliance in e-commerce.

i. [Tax-Advantaged Business Structures]: Examine various business structures and their potential tax advantages for e-commerce businesses, such as LLCs, S-corporations, and sole proprietorships.

j. [Sales Tax Updates]: Share updates and changes in sales tax laws and regulations that may impact e-commerce businesses, and offer guidance on staying informed and adapting to new requirements.

9. **International E-Commerce: Discussing strategies for expanding an e-commerce business to international markets, including language, currency, and cultural considerations.**

   a. [Expanding to International Markets]: Discuss strategies for expanding an e-commerce business to international markets, including market research, language, and cultural considerations.

   b. [Multilingual Website]: Provide guidance on creating and managing a multilingual e-commerce website, including translation, localization, and language detection techniques.

   c. [Currency and Payment Methods]: Offer advice on handling multiple currencies and payment methods for international e-commerce transactions, including conversion rates and payment gateway options.

   d. [International Shipping and Customs]: Explore the challenges and best practices for managing international shipping and customs compliance for e-commerce businesses.

   e. [Taxes and Duties]: Discuss strategies for navigating taxes, duties, and regulatory requirements when selling products to customers in different countries.

   f. [Cultural Adaptation]: Share tips for adapting e-commerce marketing and product offerings to suit the preferences and cultural norms of different international markets.

g. [Legal Considerations]: Examine legal considerations for international e-commerce businesses, such as intellectual property protection, data privacy regulations, and consumer rights.

h. [Global E-Commerce Platforms]: Provide an overview of global e-commerce platforms that support international sales and operations, including their features, benefits, and limitations.

i. [International Customer Support]: Offer guidance on providing customer support in multiple languages and time zones for e-commerce businesses operating in international markets.

j. [Localization Tools and Services]: Discuss popular localization tools and services for e-commerce businesses looking to expand internationally, including translation software and professional localization agencies.

10. **E-Commerce Analytics and Performance: Providing insights into tracking and analyzing e-commerce performance using analytics tools and data-driven decision-making.**

a. [E-Commerce Analytics Basics]: Provide an overview of e-commerce analytics, including key performance indicators (KPIs), data sources, and reporting tools.

b. [Google Analytics for E-Commerce]: Discuss the features and benefits of using Google Analytics for tracking and analyzing e-commerce performance, including setup, reporting, and advanced features.

c. [Conversion Tracking]: Share best practices for setting up and monitoring conversion tracking in e-commerce, including tracking codes, goal funnels, and attribution models.

d. [Customer Lifetime Value (CLV)]: Explore the concept of customer lifetime value and its importance in e-commerce analytics, including calculation methods and strategies for increasing CLV.

e. [E-Commerce Dashboard]: Offer guidance on creating an e-commerce dashboard to monitor and visualize key performance metrics in real-time.

f. [A/B Testing and Optimization]: Discuss the role of A/B testing in e-commerce analytics and share strategies for optimizing website elements and marketing campaigns based on data-driven insights.

g. [Customer Segmentation]: Examine the importance of customer segmentation in e-commerce analytics and share tips for creating and analyzing segments based on demographics, behavior, and other criteria.

h. [Cohort Analysis]: Explore the concept of cohort analysis and its application in e-commerce analytics, including tracking customer behavior and retention over time.

i. [Advanced E-Commerce Analytics Tools]: Provide an overview of advanced e-commerce analytics tools and platforms, including their features, pricing, and integration capabilities.

j. [Data-Driven Decision Making]: Discuss the importance of data-driven decision-making in e-commerce and share strategies for leveraging analytics insights to drive business growth and profitability.

6

Editing & Proofreading Prompts

1. **Grammar and Punctuation: Offering guidance on identifying and correcting grammar and punctuation errors in written content.**
   a. [Common Grammar Errors]: Discuss common grammar errors in written content and provide guidance on identifying and correcting them.
   b. [Punctuation Best Practices]: Offer advice on using punctuation marks correctly, including commas, semicolons, and quotation marks.
   c. [Subject-Verb Agreement]: Explore the concept of subject-verb agreement and share tips for ensuring proper agreement in sentences.
   d. [Active vs. Passive Voice]: Discuss the differences between active and passive voice and provide guidance on choosing the appropriate voice for different types of writing.

e. [Parallel Structure]: Explain the importance of parallel structure in writing and share techniques for maintaining consistency in lists and comparisons.

f. [Pronoun Usage]: Offer advice on proper pronoun usage, including antecedent agreement and avoiding ambiguous references.

g. [Verb Tense Consistency]: Provide guidance on maintaining verb tense consistency throughout a written piece, including tips for recognizing and correcting tense shifts.

h. [Modifiers and Dangling Participles]: Explore common issues with modifiers and dangling participles and share strategies for correcting them.

i. [Commonly Confused Words]: Discuss frequently confused words and provide tips for correctly using homophones, homonyms, and other similar-sounding words.

j. [Capitalization Rules]: Offer guidance on proper capitalization in written content, including titles, proper nouns, and acronyms.

2. **Spelling and Vocabulary: Providing advice on improving spelling and vocabulary usage in writing.**

a. [Spelling Tips and Tricks]: Share helpful tips and strategies for improving spelling accuracy in writing.

b. [Commonly Misspelled Words]: Discuss frequently misspelled words and provide guidance on correctly spelling them.

c. [Contextual Spelling Errors]: Offer advice on identifying and correcting contextual spelling errors, such as homophones and homonyms.

d. [Expanding Vocabulary]: Provide tips for expanding vocabulary and incorporating new words into written content.

e. [Word Choice]: Share guidance on selecting the most appropriate words to convey meaning and tone in writing.

f. [Synonyms and Antonyms]: Discuss the effective use of synonyms and antonyms to enhance vocabulary and avoid repetition in writing.

g. [Idiomatic Expressions]: Offer advice on using idiomatic expressions and colloquialisms in writing, including understanding their meanings and appropriate contexts.

h. [Jargon and Technical Terms]: Provide guidance on using jargon and technical terms in writing, including when to use them and how to define them for readers.

i. [Spelling Variations]: Explore regional spelling variations and their impact on writing for international audiences.

j. [Spelling Resources]: Share useful spelling resources and tools, such as dictionaries, spell checkers, and word games, to improve spelling accuracy.

3. **Sentence Structure and Clarity: Discussing tech-**

niques for enhancing sentence structure and clarity in written work.

a. [Basic Sentence Structure]: Provide an overview of basic sentence structure, including subjects, predicates, and objects.

b. [Complex Sentences]: Discuss the use of complex sentences in writing, including how to construct and punctuate them correctly.

c. [Sentence Variety]: Offer advice on incorporating sentence variety in writing to maintain reader interest and improve readability.

d. [Run-on Sentences]: Explore the issue of run-on sentences and provide guidance on identifying and correcting them.

e. [Sentence Fragments]: Discuss the concept of sentence fragments and share strategies for correcting incomplete sentences in writing.

f. [Parallelism in Sentences]: Offer guidance on using parallelism in sentence structure to enhance clarity and flow.

g. [Transitional Words and Phrases]: Provide tips for using transitional words and phrases to connect ideas and improve sentence flow.

h. [Eliminating Wordiness]: Share strategies for reducing wordiness and improving sentence clarity in written content.

i. [Rhetorical Devices]: Discuss the use of rhetorical devices, such as alliteration and repetition, in sentence structure and their impact on clarity and readability.

   j. [Sentence Structure Resources]: Offer useful resources and tools for improving sentence structure and clarity in writing, such as writing guides and online tutorials.

4. **Consistency and Style: Providing guidance on maintaining consistency and adhering to a specific style guide or tone throughout a written piece.**

   a. [Style Guides]: Provide an overview of common style guides and their importance in maintaining consistency in written content.

   b. [Choosing a Style Guide]: Offer advice on selecting an appropriate style guide for various types of writing projects.

   c. [Maintaining Consistency]: Discuss techniques for ensuring consistency in writing, such as using the same tense, voice, and formatting throughout a document.

   d. [Adapting to Different Writing Styles]: Share guidance on adapting to different writing styles, such as formal, informal, academic, or business writing.

   e. [Writing for a Specific Audience]: Offer advice on tailoring writing style to a specific target audience, including considering their needs and preferences.

   f. [Tone and Voice]: Provide tips for establishing

and maintaining a consistent tone and voice in written content.

g. [Formatting Consistency]: Discuss the importance of consistent formatting in writing, such as headings, font styles, and spacing.

h. [Citation Styles]: Offer guidance on using citation styles consistently and accurately in academic and research writing.

i. [Editing for Consistency]: Share strategies for editing written content to ensure consistency in style, tone, and formatting.

j. [Style Guide Resources]: Provide useful resources and tools for learning and implementing style guides in writing projects.

5. **Formatting and Layout: Offering advice on proper formatting and layout for various types of writing, such as academic papers, blog posts, and business documents.**

a. [Formatting Basics]: Discuss basic formatting principles for various types of written content, including font choices, spacing, and margins.

b. [Academic Paper Formatting]: Offer guidance on formatting academic papers, such as essays, research papers, and dissertations, according to common style guidelines.

c. [Blog Post Formatting]: Share tips for formatting blog posts to enhance readability and user engagement.

d. [Business Document Formatting]: Provide advice

on proper formatting for business documents, such as reports, proposals, and memos.

e. [E-book Formatting]: Discuss the process of formatting e-books for various platforms and devices.

f. [Accessible Formatting]: Offer guidance on creating accessible written content, including considerations for font size, color contrast, and document structure.

g. [Visual Design Elements]: Explore the use of visual design elements, such as images, tables, and graphs, to enhance the layout and presentation of written content.

h. [Citation Formatting]: Share tips for formatting citations and bibliographies according to common citation styles.

i. [Formatting Tools]: Provide information on various formatting tools and software, such as Microsoft Word, Google Docs, and LaTeX.

j. [Formatting Resources]: Offer useful resources and guides for learning proper formatting techniques and best practices in writing.

6. **Proofreading Techniques: Discussing effective proofreading techniques and strategies for identifying and correcting errors in written content.**

a. [Proofreading Process]: Discuss the importance of proofreading and provide an overview of the proofreading process.

b. [Proofreading Strategies]: Offer guidance on

effective proofreading strategies, such as reading aloud, reading backward, and using checklists.

c. [Proofreading for Spelling and Grammar]: Share tips for identifying and correcting spelling and grammar errors during the proofreading process.

d. [Proofreading for Consistency and Clarity]: Provide advice on proofreading for consistency in style, tone, and formatting, as well as ensuring clarity in writing.

e. [Proofreading for Punctuation]: Discuss techniques for identifying and correcting punctuation errors during the proofreading process.

f. [Proofreading for Typography and Formatting]: Offer guidance on proofreading for typographical and formatting errors, such as misplaced headings, inconsistent fonts, and incorrect spacing.

g. [Peer Proofreading]: Share the benefits of peer proofreading and tips for providing and receiving constructive feedback.

h. [Proofreading Tools]: Provide information on various proofreading tools and software, such as grammar checkers and spell checkers, to assist in the proofreading process.

i. [Developing Proofreading Skills]: Offer advice on improving proofreading skills, including tips for staying focused and maintaining attention to detail.

j. [Proofreading Resources]: Share useful resources

and guides for learning and refining proofreading techniques and best practices.

7. **Editing for Brevity and Conciseness: Providing guidance on trimming unnecessary words and phrases to create clear and concise writing.**

   a. [Importance of Brevity]: Discuss the importance of brevity and conciseness in written content and its impact on readability and clarity.

   b. [Eliminating Redundancy]: Offer guidance on identifying and eliminating redundant words and phrases in writing.

   c. [Trimming Wordiness]: Share tips for reducing wordiness and improving conciseness in sentences and paragraphs.

   d. [Concise Writing Techniques]: Provide advice on using concise writing techniques, such as active voice, strong verbs, and precise language.

   e. [Editing for Clarity]: Discuss strategies for editing written content to enhance clarity and remove unnecessary information.

   f. [Brevity in Different Writing Styles]: Offer guidance on achieving brevity and conciseness in various writing styles, such as academic, business, or creative writing.

   g. [Condensing Content]: Share techniques for condensing content without losing essential information or meaning.

   h. [Using Lists and Bullet Points]: Provide tips for

using lists and bullet points to convey information concisely and effectively.

i. [Brevity in Titles and Headings]: Discuss the importance of brevity and conciseness in titles and headings for improved readability and impact.

j. [Brevity and Conciseness Resources]: Offer useful resources and tools for learning and practicing brevity and conciseness in writing.

8. **Editing for Tone and Voice: Offering advice on adjusting tone and voice in writing to better align with the intended audience and purpose.**

a. [Understanding Tone and Voice]: Provide an overview of tone and voice in writing and their impact on reader engagement and comprehension.

b. [Identifying the Intended Tone and Voice]: Offer guidance on determining the appropriate tone and voice for various types of writing projects and audiences.

c. [Adjusting Tone and Voice]: Share tips for adjusting tone and voice in writing to better align with the intended audience and purpose.

d. [Formal vs. Informal Tone]: Discuss the differences between formal and informal tone and provide guidance on choosing the right tone for different situations.

e. [Persuasive Tone]: Offer advice on using a persuasive tone in writing, including techniques for building credibility and appealing to emotions.

f. [Humor and Sarcasm]: Provide tips for incorporating humor and sarcasm in writing without alienating or offending the audience.

g. [Tone and Voice in Business Writing]: Share guidance on establishing and maintaining a professional tone and voice in business communications.

h. [Tone and Voice in Creative Writing]: Discuss techniques for developing a unique and engaging tone and voice in creative writing projects.

i. [Editing for Tone and Voice Consistency]: Offer advice on editing written content to ensure tone and voice consistency throughout the piece.

j. [Tone and Voice Resources]: Provide useful resources and tools for learning and refining tone and voice in writing.

9. **Peer Review and Feedback: Discussing the benefits of peer review and offering guidance on providing constructive feedback on others' writing.**

a. [The Importance of Peer Review]: Discuss the benefits of peer review in the writing process, including improving content quality and gaining new perspectives.

b. [Conducting a Peer Review]: Offer guidance on conducting a thorough and effective peer review of another person's writing.

c. [Giving Constructive Feedback]: Share tips for providing constructive feedback on writing, including focusing on specific issues and offering suggestions for improvement.

d. [Receiving Feedback]: Provide advice on handling and processing feedback from others, including how to remain open to criticism and learn from it.

e. [Peer Review Techniques]: Offer techniques for conducting a comprehensive peer review, such as focusing on content, organization, and clarity.

f. [Collaborative Editing]: Share tips for working collaboratively with others to edit and improve written content.

g. [Peer Review in Academic Settings]: Provide guidance on participating in peer review activities in academic settings, such as workshops and writing groups.

h. [Creating a Writing Community]: Discuss the benefits of creating a writing community to facilitate peer review and feedback on an ongoing basis.

i. [Peer Review Resources]: Offer useful resources and tools for learning and refining peer review techniques and providing constructive feedback on writing.

j. [Handling Constructive Criticism]: Provide tips for gracefully receiving and implementing constructive criticism during the peer review process, and discuss the importance of being open to feedback for personal growth and improved writing skills.

10. **Editing Tools and Resources: Providing information on various editing and proofreading tools and resources, such as grammar checkers and style guides, to improve writing quality.**

    a. [Grammar and Spelling Checkers]: Discuss the benefits and limitations of using grammar and spelling checkers to improve writing quality.

    b. [Style Guide Resources]: Provide an overview of style guide resources, such as online guides and print manuals, to help maintain consistency in writing.

    c. [Writing and Editing Software]: Offer guidance on various writing and editing software options, including their features and benefits.

    d. [Online Dictionaries and Thesauri]: Share tips for using online dictionaries and thesauri to enhance vocabulary and word choice in writing.

    e. [Citation and Bibliography Tools]: Provide information on tools and software for generating citations and bibliographies according to different citation styles.

    f. [Collaborative Editing Platforms]: Discuss the benefits of using collaborative editing platforms, such as Google Docs and Microsoft Word Online, to work on writing projects with others.

    g. [Text-to-Speech Tools]: Offer advice on using

text-to-speech tools to assist with proofreading and editing written content.

h. [Writing and Editing Courses]: Share information on available writing and editing courses, both online and in-person, to improve writing skills and knowledge.

i. [Editing for Non-Native Speakers]: Provide resources and tools for non-native speakers to improve their writing and editing skills in a second language.

j. [Writing Communities and Forums]: Offer guidance on finding and participating in writing communities and forums, where writers can share resources, feedback, and support.

7

Goal Setting Prompts

1. **Setting SMART Goals: Explaining the concept of setting specific, measurable, achievable, relevant, and time-bound (SMART) goals and providing examples of how to apply this framework.**
   a. [Personal Development]: Discuss the benefits of setting SMART goals for personal development, and provide examples of specific, measurable, achievable, relevant, and time-bound goals in areas such as fitness, education, or career advancement.
   b. [Entrepreneurship]: Explain the importance of setting SMART goals when starting or growing a business, and offer examples of how to apply this framework to areas such as revenue growth, customer acquisition, or product development.
   c. [Team Management]: Discuss the role of SMART goals in team management, and provide advice

on how to set and communicate specific, measurable, achievable, relevant, and time-bound objectives to motivate and guide team members.

d. [Financial Planning]: Discuss the benefits of setting SMART goals for financial planning, and offer examples of specific, measurable, achievable, relevant, and time-bound goals, such as saving for retirement, paying off debt, or building an emergency fund.

e. [Project Management]: Explain how to use the SMART framework to set and track project goals, and provide examples of how to ensure each goal is specific, measurable, achievable, relevant, and time-bound to achieve project success.

f. [Academic Achievement]: Discuss the role of SMART goals in achieving academic success, and offer examples of specific, measurable, achievable, relevant, and time-bound goals in areas such as test scores, grade point average, or research projects.

g. [Career Development]: Explain how to apply the SMART framework to career development, and offer examples of specific, measurable, achievable, relevant, and time-bound goals such as skills development, networking, or job search strategies.

h. [Time Management]: Discuss how setting SMART goals can improve time management and productivity, and offer examples of specific, measurable, achievable, relevant, and time-bound goals in areas such as daily tasks, long-term projects, or personal hobbies.

i. [Health and Wellness]: Discuss the role of SMART goals in achieving health and wellness objectives, and offer examples of specific, measurable, achievable, relevant, and time-bound goals in areas such as fitness, nutrition, or mental health.

j. [Personal Finance]: Explain how setting SMART goals can help with personal finance management, and offer examples of specific, measurable, achievable, relevant, and time-bound goals in areas such as budgeting, debt reduction, or investment strategies.

2. **Long-term Goal Planning: Offering guidance on planning and achieving long-term goals, such as career aspirations, personal development, and financial goals.**

a. [Career Goals]: Discuss the importance of setting long-term career goals and provide tips for creating a plan to achieve them, including acquiring necessary skills and networking.

b. [Financial Planning]: Offer advice on setting and achieving long-term financial goals, such as saving for retirement or paying off debt, including strategies for budgeting and investing.

c. [Personal Development]: Discuss the benefits of setting long-term personal development goals and provide tips for achieving them, such as pursuing education or developing new skills.

d. [Entrepreneurship]: Offer guidance on setting and achieving long-term entrepreneurial goals, such as launching a successful startup or growing a small business, including developing a business plan and networking.

e. [Health and Fitness]: Discuss the importance of setting long-term health and fitness goals and provide tips for achieving them, such as creating a workout plan and adopting a healthy diet.

f. [Travel and Adventure]: Offer advice on setting and achieving long-term travel and adventure goals, such as visiting all seven continents or completing a hiking challenge, including budgeting and planning logistics.

g. [Relationship Goals]: Discuss the benefits of setting long-term relationship goals, such as improving communication or strengthening a partnership, and provide tips for achieving them.

h. [Volunteering and Community Service]: Offer guidance on setting and achieving long-term volunteering and community service goals, such as joining a nonprofit board or completing a service project, including finding opportunities and making a plan.

i. [Artistic and Creative Pursuits]: Discuss the importance of setting long-term artistic and creative goals, such as writing a novel or painting a series of artworks, and provide tips for achieving them, such as setting deadlines and collaborating with others.

j. [Education and Learning]: Offer advice on setting and achieving long-term education and learning goals, such as earning a degree or mastering a new language, including creating a study plan and seeking out resources.

3. **Short-term Goal Planning: Providing tips for setting and achieving short-term goals, such as daily and weekly objectives, to build momentum and progress towards long-term goals.**

a. [Productivity]: Explain the importance of setting short-term goals to increase productivity and offer tips for breaking down larger projects into smaller, achievable tasks.

b. [Fitness]: Discuss the benefits of setting short-term fitness goals, such as running a certain distance or lifting a certain weight, and provide tips for tracking progress and staying motivated.

c. [Financial Planning]: Provide guidance on setting short-term financial goals, such as saving a certain amount of money each week or paying off a credit card balance, and offer tips for budgeting and managing expenses.

d. [Academic Success]: Offer advice on setting and achieving short-term academic goals, such as completing a certain number of readings or mastering a specific topic, to improve overall performance and build momentum.

e. [Personal Development]: Discuss the importance of setting short-term goals for personal growth and provide tips for identifying areas of improvement, such as learning a new skill or practicing a hobby.

f. [Career Development]: Provide guidance on setting short-term career goals, such as completing a training program or networking with industry professionals, to advance in a chosen field.

g. [Health and Wellness]: Offer advice on setting short-term health goals, such as drinking a certain amount of water each day or getting a certain amount of sleep each night, to improve overall wellness.

h. [Time Management]: Discuss how setting daily and weekly goals can improve time management and productivity, and offer tips for prioritizing tasks and avoiding distractions.

i. [Relationship Building]: Provide guidance on setting short-term relationship goals, such as spending quality time with loved ones or reaching out to a friend, to strengthen connections and build meaningful relationships.

j. [Habit Formation]: Discuss the importance of setting short-term goals for forming new habits, such as practicing mindfulness or exercising daily, and offer tips for tracking progress and staying motivated.

4. **Goal Visualization and Affirmations: Sharing techniques for visualizing and affirming goals, such as creating vision boards and positive self-talk, to increase motivation and focus.**

   a. [Mindset]: Discuss the importance of a positive mindset in achieving goals, and offer techniques for creating affirmations that support this mindset.

   b. [Visual Aids]: Explain the benefits of using visual aids, such as vision boards or mind maps, to help visualize and achieve goals, and provide examples of how to create these aids.

   c. [Daily Practice]: Share tips for incorporating daily goal visualization and affirmation practices into a busy schedule, such as meditation or journaling.

   d. [Motivation]: Discuss how goal visualization and affirmations can increase motivation and provide techniques for staying motivated when facing obstacles or setbacks.

   e. [Accountability]: Offer strategies for holding oneself accountable for achieving goals, such as sharing progress with a friend or mentor, and incorporating accountability into daily goal visualization and affirmation practices.

   f. [Personal Growth]: Discuss how goal visualization and affirmations can support personal growth and offer techniques for creating affirmations that focus on personal development.

g. [Visualization Techniques]: Share different visualization techniques, such as guided imagery or mental rehearsal, that can be used to support goal visualization and manifestation.

h. [Positive Self-Talk]: Discuss the importance of positive self-talk in achieving goals and offer techniques for creating affirmations that reinforce positive self-talk.

i. [Emotional Connection]: Explain the benefits of creating an emotional connection to goals and offer techniques for incorporating emotions into goal visualization and affirmations.

j. [Long-term Success]: Share strategies for using goal visualization and affirmations to achieve long-term success, such as creating a long-term vision board or incorporating affirmations into a daily success routine.

5. **Overcoming Obstacles and Setbacks: Discussing common obstacles and setbacks that can impede goal achievement, such as procrastination and self-doubt, and offering strategies for overcoming them.**

a. [Perseverance]: Explain the importance of persistence in achieving goals, and share strategies for staying motivated and focused during challenging times.

b. [Mindset]: Discuss the impact of mindset on goal achievement, including the role of self-talk and mindset shifts in overcoming obstacles and setbacks.

c. [Accountability]: Explain the benefits of accountability in goal setting and share techniques for holding oneself accountable, such as setting deadlines and tracking progress.

d. [Self-Reflection]: Discuss the importance of self-reflection in goal setting and achievement, and share techniques for identifying areas for improvement and adapting goals as needed.

e. [Fear]: Discuss the role of fear in goal achievement, including common fears such as failure and rejection, and share techniques for overcoming them.

f. [Positive Habits]: Explain how developing positive habits can support goal achievement, and share strategies for building and maintaining healthy habits.

g. [Support System]: Discuss the importance of a support system in goal achievement, including the role of mentors, friends, and family, and share tips for building a strong support network.

h. [Growth Mindset]: Discuss the benefits of a growth mindset in goal achievement, including the ability to learn from mistakes and embrace challenges, and share techniques for cultivating a growth mindset.

i. [Time Management]: Discuss the impact of time management on goal achievement, including the importance of prioritization and effective use of time, and share strategies for optimizing time management.

j. [Resilience]: Explain the importance of resilience in goal achievement, including the ability to bounce back from setbacks and adapt to change, and share techniques for building resilience.

6. **Accountability and Tracking Progress: Recommending methods for holding oneself accountable and tracking progress towards goals, such as journaling and using apps and tools.**

a. [Habit Formation]: Discuss the importance of forming new habits when working towards achieving goals, and recommend methods for tracking and holding oneself accountable to new habits.

b. [Self-Motivation]: Provide advice on how to maintain self-motivation when working towards long-term goals, and recommend methods for tracking progress and celebrating milestones.

c. [Mental Health]: Discuss the impact of mental health on goal achievement, and provide tips for self-care and seeking support when facing setbacks or challenges.

d. [Team Accountability]: Offer advice on setting and achieving goals as a team, and recommend methods for holding team members accountable to individual and group goals.

e. [Feedback]: Discuss the importance of feedback

in goal achievement, and provide tips for seeking and receiving constructive feedback to improve performance.

f. [Reflection]: Recommend methods for reflecting on progress towards goals, and discuss the benefits of regular reflection in achieving success.

g. [Visualization]: Offer techniques for visualizing progress towards goals, and discuss the benefits of incorporating visualization into goal-setting and tracking.

h. [Time Management]: Discuss the role of time management in achieving goals, and recommend methods for tracking and managing time effectively to optimize productivity.

i. [Rewards]: Discuss the role of rewards in maintaining motivation and achieving goals, and recommend methods for setting and achieving reward-based milestones.

j. [Goal Maintenance]: Offer advice on maintaining long-term goals, and recommend methods for monitoring progress and adjusting goals as needed to ensure continued success.

7. **Goal Refinement and Adjustment: Offering advice on refining and adjusting goals as circumstances change, such as adjusting timelines or modifying objectives.**

a. [Career Development]: Discuss the importance of refining and adjusting career goals as one gains experience and skills, and offer tips for updating career objectives and plans accordingly.

b. [Personal Growth]: Explain the benefits of regularly refining and adjusting personal goals, and provide guidance on how to reassess and modify goals to reflect changing priorities and interests.

c. [Business Planning]: Discuss the role of goal refinement and adjustment in successful business planning, and offer strategies for revising business goals and plans based on market trends and customer feedback.

d. [Financial Planning]: Share the importance of regularly reviewing and adjusting financial goals, and provide tips for modifying financial plans to reflect changing circumstances and priorities.

e. [Fitness and Health]: Offer advice on adjusting fitness and health goals as one's physical abilities and needs change over time, and provide examples of how to modify exercise and nutrition plans accordingly.

f. [Education]: Discuss the importance of refining and adjusting educational goals as one progresses through different stages of learning, and provide guidance on how to modify academic goals and plans as needed.

g. [Relationships]: Explain the role of goal refinement and adjustment in maintaining healthy and fulfilling relationships, and offer tips for modifying relationship goals and plans based on changing circumstances and needs.

h. [Hobbies and Interests]: Share the benefits of regularly refining and adjusting goals related to hobbies and interests, and provide guidance on how to reassess and modify goals to reflect changing passions and aspirations.

i. [Travel]: Discuss the importance of refining and adjusting travel goals as one gains new experiences and discovers new destinations, and provide tips for modifying travel plans to reflect changing interests and priorities.

j. [Community Involvement]: Offer advice on adjusting goals related to community involvement and volunteer work, and provide examples of how to modify plans and objectives based on changing needs and opportunities.

8. **Goal Setting for Teams and Organizations: Sharing tips for setting and achieving goals as a team or organization, including alignment of goals and effective communication.**

a. [Team Alignment]: Discuss the importance of aligning team and organizational goals with the company's mission and vision, and provide tips for ensuring all team members understand and prioritize these goals.

b. [Effective Communication]: Discuss how effective communication can improve team goal setting and achievement, and offer strategies for fostering open communication and collaboration within a team.

c. [Measurement and Evaluation]: Discuss the importance of measuring and evaluating progress towards team goals, and offer tips for using data to track progress and make adjustments as needed.

d. [Goal Prioritization]: Discuss how to prioritize team goals based on importance and urgency, and offer strategies for allocating resources and managing competing priorities.

e. [Accountability and Responsibility]: Discuss the importance of individual accountability and responsibility for achieving team goals, and offer tips for holding team members accountable and incentivizing goal achievement.

f. [Collaborative Goal Setting]: Discuss the benefits of collaborative goal setting and involve all team members in the process, and offer tips for facilitating productive discussions and reaching consensus.

g. [Long-Term Goal Planning]: Discuss the importance of long-term goal planning for teams and organizations, and offer tips for breaking down long-term goals into smaller, achievable milestones.

h. [SMART Goals]: Discuss how the SMART goal framework can be applied to team and organizational goal setting, and offer examples of specific, measurable, achievable, relevant, and time-bound goals for different teams and departments.

    i. [Motivation and Recognition]: Discuss how motivation and recognition can improve team goal achievement, and offer strategies for rewarding team members and maintaining morale.

    j. [Goal Setting for Remote Teams]: Discuss unique challenges and opportunities of goal setting for remote teams, and offer tips for maintaining alignment, communication, and accountability in a virtual work environment.

9. **Goal Setting for Personal Wellness: Providing guidance on setting and achieving goals related to personal wellness, such as fitness, mental health, and self-care.**

    a. [Fitness]: Discuss the importance of setting SMART goals for fitness and provide tips for creating specific and achievable goals for cardio, strength training, and flexibility exercises.

    b. [Mental Health]: Offer guidance on setting and achieving mental health goals, such as meditation, therapy, or journaling, and discuss the benefits of a consistent self-care routine.

    c. [Nutrition]: Discuss the role of goal setting in developing healthy eating habits and offer tips for setting goals that are realistic, measurable, and aligned with individual dietary needs and preferences.

    d. [Sleep]: Discuss the importance of setting goals

for improving sleep quality and quantity, and provide tips for creating a bedtime routine, setting sleep goals, and tracking progress.

e. [Self-care]: Offer guidance on setting goals for self-care, such as taking breaks, practicing mindfulness, or indulging in hobbies, and discuss the benefits of a consistent self-care routine.

f. [Stress Management]: Discuss the role of goal setting in managing stress and provide tips for creating achievable goals for stress reduction techniques, such as exercise, meditation, or deep breathing exercises.

g. [Time Management]: Discuss how setting goals for personal wellness can improve time management and productivity, and offer examples of specific, measurable, achievable, relevant, and time-bound goals in areas such as exercise, sleep, and self-care.

h. [Accountability]: Discuss the importance of accountability in achieving personal wellness goals and provide tips for holding oneself accountable, such as tracking progress, setting reminders, or seeking support from friends or family.

i. [Motivation]: Offer guidance on maintaining motivation and momentum when working towards personal wellness goals, and discuss the benefits of celebrating small victories and rewarding oneself for progress.

j. [Habit Formation]: Discuss the role of goal

setting in forming healthy habits for personal wellness, such as exercise, nutrition, and self-care, and provide tips for creating and maintaining habits that support overall well-being.

10. **Goal Setting for Creatives: Discussing unique considerations for setting and achieving goals for creative pursuits, such as writing, art, and music, and providing tips for staying motivated and overcoming creative blocks.**

    a. [Creative Productivity]: Share tips for setting and achieving creative goals, such as writing a novel or producing an album, and discuss the importance of establishing a routine and tracking progress.

    b. [Overcoming Creative Blocks]: Discuss common creative blocks, such as writer's block or artist's block, and offer strategies for overcoming them, such as brainstorming and taking breaks.

    c. [Goal Refinement for Creatives]: Offer advice on refining and adjusting creative goals as projects evolve or circumstances change, such as revising a manuscript or modifying a performance.

    d. [Goal Visualization for Creatives]: Share techniques for visualizing and manifesting creative goals, such as creating a vision board or using positive affirmations, to enhance motivation and focus.

    e. [Collaborative Goal Setting for Creatives]: Discuss the benefits and challenges of setting goals as a creative team or group, and provide strategies for aligning individual goals with shared objectives.

f. [Goal Setting for Creative Entrepreneurs]: Share advice on setting and achieving business goals as a creative entrepreneur, such as launching a product line or expanding a client base, and discuss the importance of balancing creativity and strategy.

g. [Tracking Creative Progress]: Recommend tools and methods for tracking creative progress, such as project management software or daily journals, to monitor productivity and celebrate milestones.

h. [Goal Setting for Creative Self-Discovery]: Offer guidance on setting and achieving goals for personal growth and self-discovery through creative pursuits, such as journaling or art therapy.

i. [Goal Accountability for Creatives]: Share strategies for holding oneself accountable to creative goals, such as finding an accountability partner or joining a creative community, to enhance motivation and commitment.

j. [Goal Setting for Creative Wellness]: Provide advice on setting and achieving goals related to creative wellness, such as maintaining a healthy work-life balance or cultivating a positive mindset, to support long-term creative success.

8

Graphic Design Prompts

1. **Design Principles: Discussing the fundamental principles of graphic design, such as balance, hierarchy, and contrast.**
   a. [Balance]: Explain the importance of balance in graphic design and provide examples of how it can be achieved through symmetrical or asymmetrical compositions.
   b. [Hierarchy]: Discuss how the use of hierarchy in design can guide the viewer's attention and suggest techniques such as varying font size or using color contrast.
   c. [Contrast]: Analyze how contrast can create visual interest in design and recommend techniques such as using complementary colors or varying line weight.
   d. [Color Theory]: Explain the principles of color theory in design and suggest ways to use color

effectively to communicate meaning and evoke emotion.

e. [Typography]: Discuss the role of typography in design and recommend techniques such as choosing appropriate font styles and pairing complementary typefaces.

f. [White Space]: Analyze how white space can enhance design and suggest techniques such as using negative space to create a sense of balance and focus.

g. [Grid Systems]: Explain the benefits of using grid systems in design and suggest techniques such as using the rule of thirds or the golden ratio.

h. [Visual Hierarchy]: Discuss how visual hierarchy can be used to organize information in design and recommend techniques such as using size, color, or shape to indicate importance.

i. [Composition]: Analyze how the principles of composition, such as rule of thirds or symmetry, can be used to create visually appealing designs and suggest techniques for achieving balance and harmony.

j. [Accessibility]: Discuss how graphic design can be made accessible to individuals with disabilities and recommend techniques such as using high contrast colors or appropriate font size.

2. **Typography: Exploring various aspects of typography, including font selection, pairing, and layout.**

a. [Font Selection]: Discuss the importance of font

selection in design and recommend techniques for choosing appropriate fonts for different purposes and contexts.

b. [Typography Trends]: Analyze current typography trends and discuss their impact on design and branding, and recommend how to stay up to date with these trends.

c. [Pairing Fonts]: Explain the principles of font pairing in design and recommend techniques for combining complementary and contrasting fonts.

d. [Layout]: Discuss how the layout of text can affect the readability and impact of design and recommend techniques for creating effective and engaging layouts.

e. [Serif vs Sans-Serif]: Analyze the differences between serif and sans-serif fonts and recommend techniques for choosing between them based on design context and brand identity.

f. [Custom Fonts]: Discuss the benefits and challenges of using custom fonts in design and recommend techniques for creating and integrating them effectively.

g. [Hierarchy]: Analyze how typography can be used to establish visual hierarchy in design and recommend techniques for creating effective hierarchies through font selection, sizing, and placement.

h. [Legibility]: Discuss the importance of legibility

in design and recommend techniques for improving legibility through font selection, size, and spacing.

   i. [Color]: Analyze how color can be used in typography to create visual interest and impact and recommend techniques for choosing and using color effectively.

   j. [Accessibility]: Discuss the importance of accessibility in typography and recommend techniques for creating designs that are readable and accessible to individuals with visual impairments.

3. **Color Theory: Offering guidance on color selection, combinations, and the emotional impact of different hues.**

   a. [Color Wheel]: Explain the principles of the color wheel in design and recommend techniques for choosing complementary and contrasting color combinations.

   b. [Color Psychology]: Discuss the emotional impact of different colors and recommend techniques for using color to evoke specific moods and emotions in design.

   c. [Color Trends]: Analyze current color trends in design and discuss their impact on branding and visual identity.

   d. [Color Harmony]: Discuss the importance of color harmony in design and recommend techniques for creating cohesive and harmonious color palettes.

e. [Color Contrast]: Explain the principles of color contrast in design and recommend techniques for using contrast to create visual interest and impact.

f. [Color Meaning]: Analyze the symbolic meaning of different colors and recommend techniques for using color to convey meaning and message in design.

g. [Color Schemes]: Discuss the different types of color schemes, such as monochromatic, analogous, and triadic, and recommend techniques for using them effectively in design.

h. [Color in Branding]: Analyze the role of color in branding and recommend techniques for choosing colors that reflect brand identity and resonate with the target audience.

i. [Color in Typography]: Discuss the use of color in typography and recommend techniques for using color to enhance readability and hierarchy in design.

j. [Accessibility]: Discuss the importance of color accessibility in design and recommend techniques for ensuring that designs are readable and accessible to individuals with color vision deficiencies.

4. **Logo Design: Providing advice on creating effective and memorable logos for brands and businesses.**

a. [Brand Identity]: Discuss the importance of logo design in establishing brand identity and recommend techniques for creating logos that reflect the brand's values and message.

b. [Simplicity]: Analyze the benefits of simple and minimalist logo design and recommend techniques for creating effective logos that are memorable and timeless.

c. [Color]: Discuss the use of color in logo design and recommend techniques for choosing and using color effectively to enhance brand identity and recognition.

d. [Typography]: Explain the role of typography in logo design and recommend techniques for choosing and pairing fonts that complement the logo's design and message.

e. [Visual Symbolism]: Discuss the use of visual symbolism in logo design and recommend techniques for creating effective logos that convey a message or idea visually.

f. [Scalability]: Analyze the importance of scalability in logo design and recommend techniques for creating logos that are versatile and can be used across different platforms and mediums.

g. [Competitive Analysis]: Discuss the importance of researching and analyzing competitor logos and recommend techniques for creating logos that stand out in a crowded market.

h. [Target Audience]: Explain the importance of considering the target audience in logo design and recommend techniques for creating logos that resonate with the intended audience.

    i. [Testing and Iteration]: Analyze the benefits of testing and iterating logo designs and recommend techniques for gathering feedback and making improvements.

    j. [Legal Considerations]: Discuss the legal considerations in logo design, such as copyright and trademark, and recommend techniques for ensuring that logos are original and legally protected.

5. **Print Design: Discussing best practices for designing print materials, such as brochures, business cards, and posters.**

    a. [Layout]: Discuss the principles of layout design for print materials and recommend techniques for creating effective and engaging layouts.

    b. [Typography]: Analyze the role of typography in print design and recommend techniques for choosing and pairing fonts that enhance readability and visual impact.

    c. [Color]: Discuss the use of color in print design and recommend techniques for choosing and using color effectively to enhance visual appeal and readability.

    d. [Resolution]: Explain the importance of resolution in print design and recommend techniques for ensuring that designs are high-quality and print-ready.

e. [Bleed and Margins]: Discuss the importance of bleed and margins in print design and recommend techniques for ensuring that designs are correctly aligned and fit the intended print medium.

f. [Paper and Material Selection]: Analyze the impact of paper and material selection on print design and recommend techniques for choosing materials that enhance the visual impact and tactile experience of the design.

g. [Visual Hierarchy]: Discuss the importance of visual hierarchy in print design and recommend techniques for creating effective hierarchies that guide the reader's attention.

h. [Call to Action]: Analyze the importance of including a call to action in print design and recommend techniques for creating effective and persuasive calls to action.

i. [Brand Consistency]: Discuss the importance of brand consistency in print design and recommend techniques for ensuring that print materials reflect and enhance the brand's visual identity.

j. [Testing and Proofing]: Analyze the benefits of testing and proofing print designs and recommend techniques for ensuring that designs are error-free and high-quality before printing.

6. **Digital Design: Offering tips and techniques for designing digital assets, such as websites, social media graphics, and email newsletters.**

a. [User Experience]: Discuss the importance of user experience in digital design and recommend techniques for creating intuitive and engaging digital assets.

b. [Responsive Design]: Analyze the benefits of responsive design in digital assets and recommend techniques for creating designs that adapt to different screen sizes and devices.

c. [Color]: Discuss the use of color in digital design and recommend techniques for choosing and using color effectively to enhance visual appeal and readability.

d. [Typography]: Explain the role of typography in digital design and recommend techniques for choosing and pairing fonts that enhance readability and visual impact.

e. [Visual Hierarchy]: Analyze the importance of visual hierarchy in digital design and recommend techniques for creating effective hierarchies that guide the user's attention.

f. [Brand Consistency]: Discuss the importance of brand consistency in digital design and recommend techniques for ensuring that digital assets reflect and enhance the brand's visual identity.

g. [Accessibility]: Analyze the importance of accessibility in digital design and recommend techniques for ensuring that designs are readable and accessible to individuals with disabilities.

h. [Call to Action]: Discuss the importance of

including a call to action in digital assets and recommend techniques for creating effective and persuasive calls to action.

i. [Testing and Analytics]: Analyze the benefits of testing and analytics in digital design and recommend techniques for gathering feedback and using data to make design improvements.

j. [Social Media]: Discuss the unique considerations in designing digital assets for social media and recommend techniques for creating designs that are visually appealing and effective in the social media context.

7. **Design Software: Recommending and providing guidance on various design software and tools.**

a. [Adobe Creative Cloud]: Analyze the benefits of Adobe Creative Cloud and recommend techniques for using various tools, such as Photoshop, Illustrator, and InDesign, effectively.

b. [Sketch]: Discuss the features and benefits of Sketch and recommend techniques for using the tool for web and UI design.

c. [Figma]: Analyze the benefits of Figma and recommend techniques for using the tool for collaborative design and prototyping.

d. [Canva]: Discuss the features and benefits of Canva and recommend techniques for using the tool for creating graphics and visual content.

e. [Procreate]: Analyze the benefits of Procreate

and recommend techniques for using the tool for digital illustration and painting.

f. [Affinity Designer]: Discuss the features and benefits of Affinity Designer and recommend techniques for using the tool for vector design and illustration.

g. [Gravit Designer]: Analyze the benefits of Gravit Designer and recommend techniques for using the tool for vector design and illustration.

h. [Inkscape]: Discuss the features and benefits of Inkscape and recommend techniques for using the tool for vector design and illustration.

i. [Blender]: Analyze the benefits of Blender and recommend techniques for using the tool for 3D modeling and animation.

j. [AutoCAD]: Discuss the features and benefits of AutoCAD and recommend techniques for using the tool for architecture and engineering design.

8. **Branding and Identity: Exploring the role of graphic design in creating cohesive and recognizable brand identities.**

a. [Brand Identity]: Discuss the importance of brand identity in graphic design and recommend techniques for creating logos, color palettes, and typography that reflect and enhance the brand's values and message.

b. [Consistency]: Analyze the benefits of consistency in brand identity and recommend techniques for creating cohesive and recognizable visual identities across different platforms and mediums.

c. [Visual Storytelling]: Discuss the role of visual storytelling in brand identity and recommend techniques for using graphic design to tell the brand's story and create emotional connections with the audience.

d. [Brand Guidelines]: Explain the importance of brand guidelines in graphic design and recommend techniques for creating comprehensive and easy-to-follow guidelines for the brand's visual identity.

e. [Target Audience]: Analyze the importance of considering the target audience in brand identity and recommend techniques for creating visual identities that resonate with and appeal to the intended audience.

f. [Competitive Analysis]: Discuss the importance of researching and analyzing competitors' brand identities and recommend techniques for creating visual identities that stand out and differentiate the brand in a crowded market.

g. [Evolution]: Analyze the benefits of evolving and updating the brand's visual identity over time and recommend techniques for making changes that maintain brand recognition and consistency.

h. [Emotional Impact]: Discuss the importance of creating a strong emotional impact through brand identity and recommend techniques for using color, typography, and visual symbolism to create emotional connections with the audience.

    i. [Brand Voice]: Analyze the role of brand voice in graphic design and recommend techniques for creating visual identities that reflect the brand's tone and personality.

    j. [Measuring Success]: Discuss the importance of measuring the success of brand identity in graphic design and recommend techniques for using analytics and feedback to make improvements and adjustments over time.

9. **Design Critiques: Engaging in constructive critiques and analysis of graphic design work.**

    a. [Visual Analysis]: Analyze the visual elements of a design, such as color, typography, and layout, and provide constructive feedback for improving the design's impact and effectiveness.

    b. [Brand Consistency]: Evaluate a design's consistency with the brand's visual identity and provide suggestions for improving brand recognition and consistency.

    c. [User Experience]: Analyze the user experience of a design, such as navigation and accessibility, and provide suggestions for improving usability and engagement.

    d. [Communication]: Evaluate the effectiveness of a design in communicating its message or purpose and provide suggestions for improving clarity and impact.

e. [Design Process]: Discuss the design process behind a particular design and provide feedback on the effectiveness of the process and areas for improvement.

f. [Target Audience]: Evaluate a design's effectiveness in appealing to and engaging the intended target audience and provide suggestions for improving audience resonance.

g. [Design Trends]: Analyze current design trends and their impact on the design being critiqued and provide suggestions for incorporating or avoiding trends in a relevant and effective way.

h. [Visual Hierarchy]: Evaluate the use of visual hierarchy in a design and provide feedback on its effectiveness in guiding the viewer's attention and creating a clear hierarchy of information.

i. [Creativity]: Evaluate the creativity and originality of a design and provide suggestions for pushing the boundaries and exploring new ideas.

j. [Personal Growth]: Discuss personal growth opportunities for the designer based on the feedback provided and provide suggestions for continued growth and development in the field of graphic design.

10. **Design Inspiration: Recommending resources and strategies for finding design inspiration and staying current with design trends.**

a. [Online Resources]: Recommend online resources for finding design inspiration, such as design blogs, social media accounts, and design websites, and discuss the benefits of using these resources.

b. [Design Communities]: Discuss the benefits of joining design communities, such as online forums and local design groups, and recommend techniques for building relationships and finding inspiration within these communities.

c. [Magazines and Publications]: Recommend design magazines and publications that offer inspiration and insight into current design trends and discuss the benefits of staying up-to-date with industry publications.

d. [Creative Exercises]: Recommend creative exercises and prompts for generating design ideas and discuss the benefits of practicing creativity regularly.

e. [Nature and Environment]: Discuss the benefits of finding inspiration in nature and the environment and recommend techniques for incorporating natural elements into design work.

f. [Art and Photography]: Recommend art and photography resources for finding inspiration and discuss the benefits of using these mediums to inform design work.

g. [Travel and Culture]: Discuss the benefits of finding inspiration in travel and different cultures and recommend techniques for incorporating cultural elements into design work.

    h. [Personal Experience]: Discuss the benefits of finding inspiration in personal experience and recommend techniques for reflecting personal experiences in design work.

    i. [Collaboration]: Discuss the benefits of collaboration in finding design inspiration and recommend techniques for finding and collaborating with other designers and creatives.

    j. [Iteration and Experimentation]: Discuss the benefits of iteration and experimentation in finding design inspiration and recommend techniques for pushing the boundaries and exploring new ideas.

9

Personal Finance Advice Prompts

1. **Budgeting: Offering guidance on creating and maintaining a personal budget.**
   a. [Debt Reduction]: Analyze different debt reduction strategies and explain their effectiveness in achieving financial stability. Provide tips for choosing the best debt reduction method for individual circumstances.
   b. [Emergency Fund]: Discuss the importance of having an emergency fund and provide strategies for building and maintaining one. Analyze different options for saving and investing money in an emergency fund.
   c. [Saving Goals]: Explore the benefits of setting saving goals and provide strategies for achieving them. Discuss the importance of prioritizing financial goals and offer tips for staying motivated.

d. [Credit Scores]: Analyze the factors that impact credit scores and provide tips for improving them. Discuss the importance of monitoring credit reports and maintaining a good credit score.

e. [Investing]: Discuss different types of investment options and analyze their potential risks and rewards. Provide tips for creating an investment portfolio and managing risk.

f. [Retirement Planning]: Offer guidance on planning for retirement, including calculating retirement needs, selecting retirement accounts, and creating a retirement income strategy.

g. [Insurance]: Discuss different types of insurance and their importance in achieving financial stability. Provide guidance on choosing the right insurance policies and ensuring adequate coverage.

h. [Tax Planning]: Analyze different tax planning strategies and offer advice on minimizing tax liabilities. Discuss the importance of tax planning and provide tips for maximizing tax benefits.

i. [Financial Planning for Families]: Offer guidance on creating a financial plan for families, including setting financial goals, managing expenses, and creating a long-term financial strategy. Discuss the importance of communication and cooperation in achieving financial stability.

j. [Financial Literacy]: Explore the importance of financial literacy and offer tips for improving financial knowledge and skills. Discuss the benefits of financial education and offer resources for improving financial literacy.

2. **Saving & Investing: Providing advice on various saving and investment strategies.**

    a. [Debt vs. Investment]: Analyze the debate surrounding whether to prioritize paying off debt or investing for the future. Explain the pros and cons of each approach and offer advice on making the best decision for individual circumstances.

    b. [Risk Management]: Discuss the different types of investment risks and how to mitigate them. Analyze the common misconceptions surrounding risk and offer alternative perspectives.

    c. [Diversification]: Explain the importance of diversifying investments and how to effectively spread out risk. Analyze common myths surrounding diversification and provide alternative strategies.

    d. [Real Estate Investing]: Discuss the pros and cons of investing in real estate and offer advice on how to make smart decisions in the real estate market.

    e. [Retirement Planning]: Offer guidance on planning for retirement and making the most of retirement savings accounts. Analyze common retirement planning mistakes and offer alternative strategies.

    f. [Investing in Stocks]: Analyze the debate

surrounding investing in individual stocks versus index funds. Explain the risks and potential rewards of each approach and offer advice on how to make informed decisions.

g. [Alternative Investments]: Discuss the pros and cons of alternative investments such as cryptocurrencies, commodities, and art. Offer guidance on how to navigate these markets and make informed decisions.

h. [Timing the Market]: Analyze the common myth of "timing the market" and the potential risks of trying to predict market trends. Offer alternative strategies for successful investing.

i. [Socially Responsible Investing]: Explain the concept of socially responsible investing and the potential impact of investing choices on social and environmental issues. Offer guidance on how to incorporate social responsibility into investment strategies.

j. [Financial Advisors]: Discuss the pros and cons of working with a financial advisor and how to choose the right advisor for individual needs. Analyze common misconceptions surrounding financial advisors and offer alternative perspectives.

3. **Debt Management: Assisting with strategies for managing and reducing debt.**
   a. [Pros and Cons]: Analyze the pros and cons of different debt management strategies, such as

debt consolidation or debt settlement. Discuss the potential benefits and drawbacks of each approach and offer advice on which may be best suited for different situations.

b. [Budgeting for Debt]: Discuss the importance of budgeting for debt management and offer advice on how to create a budget that includes debt repayment goals. Provide tips for staying on track with debt payments and avoiding unnecessary expenses.

c. [Credit Scores]: Explain how credit scores can impact debt management and offer tips for improving credit scores. Discuss how to monitor credit reports and address any errors or discrepancies.

d. [Negotiating with Creditors]: Discuss strategies for negotiating with creditors to reduce interest rates, lower payments, or settle debts. Offer advice on how to approach these conversations and what to consider before agreeing to any terms.

e. [Debt Relief Programs]: Analyze the pros and cons of debt relief programs, such as debt management plans or debt settlement programs. Explain how these programs work and discuss the potential impact on credit scores and overall financial health.

f. [Prioritizing Debt]: Discuss how to prioritize debt repayment, including strategies for paying off high-interest debts first or focusing on debts with the smallest balances. Offer advice on how to balance debt repayment with other financial goals, such as saving for retirement.

g. [Debt Consolidation]: Discuss the pros and cons of debt consolidation, including using personal loans, balance transfer credit cards, or home equity loans. Offer advice on when debt consolidation may be a good option and how to avoid potential pitfalls.

h. [Avoiding Debt]: Offer advice on how to avoid accumulating debt in the first place. Discuss strategies for living within one's means, avoiding unnecessary expenses, and building an emergency fund.

i. [Managing Student Loans]: Discuss strategies for managing student loan debt, including loan consolidation, income-driven repayment plans, or refinancing. Offer advice on how to balance student loan payments with other financial goals.

j. [Seeking Professional Help]: Discuss when it may be necessary to seek professional help for debt management, such as working with a financial advisor or credit counselor. Offer advice on how to find reputable professionals and what to expect from their services.

4. **Credit Score Improvement: Offering tips on improving credit scores and maintaining good credit.**

a. [Expert Opinion]: Discuss the most effective methods for improving a credit score according to financial experts. Provide examples of successful cases and explain the reasoning behind the recommended strategies.

b. [Myth Busting]: Identify common misconceptions about credit scores and credit reports. Explain why these myths are incorrect and provide evidence to support your argument.

c. [Comparative Analysis]: Compare and contrast different credit score monitoring services. Analyze the features, pricing, and overall value of each service and recommend the best option for improving credit scores.

d. [Case Study]: Provide a case study of someone who has successfully improved their credit score. Analyze the steps they took, the mistakes they avoided, and offer recommendations for others looking to follow a similar path.

e. [Cost-Benefit Analysis]: Offer a cost-benefit analysis of paying off debt versus investing in assets that can improve credit scores. Discuss the long-term benefits and potential drawbacks of each approach.

f. [Debate]: Host a debate between two experts with different opinions on credit score improvement. Analyze the arguments of each expert and provide a synthesis of their viewpoints.

g. [Personal Experience]: Share your own personal experience of improving your credit score. Discuss the methods you used and the challenges you faced. Offer advice to others looking to improve their credit score.

h. [Legal Considerations]: Discuss the legal considerations that people should be aware of when trying to improve their credit scores. Explain the rules and regulations surrounding credit reporting and offer tips for navigating these laws.

i. [Psychological Factors]: Explore the psychological factors that influence people's ability to improve their credit scores. Discuss the impact of motivation, discipline, and mindset on credit score improvement.

j. [Technology]: Discuss the role of technology in credit score improvement. Analyze the latest technological advancements in credit monitoring and provide recommendations for people looking to leverage technology to improve their credit scores.

5. **Retirement Planning: Providing guidance on planning for a secure financial future.**

a. [Pros and Cons]: Discuss the pros and cons of different retirement planning strategies and provide recommendations for the most effective approach.

b. [Long-Term Goals]: Discuss the importance of setting long-term financial goals for retirement planning and offer advice on creating a realistic plan to achieve those goals.

c. [Risk Assessment]: Analyze the risks involved in

retirement planning and offer strategies for managing those risks, including diversification and asset allocation.

d. [Savings Strategies]: Offer advice on developing effective savings strategies for retirement planning, including maximizing contributions to retirement accounts and minimizing debt.

e. [Social Security]: Discuss the role of Social Security in retirement planning and provide advice on how to optimize Social Security benefits.

f. [Healthcare Costs]: Address the impact of healthcare costs on retirement planning and offer strategies for managing those costs, including long-term care insurance and health savings accounts.

g. [Inflation]: Analyze the impact of inflation on retirement planning and offer strategies for managing inflation risk, such as investing in inflation-protected securities.

h. [Tax Planning]: Discuss the importance of tax planning in retirement and offer strategies for minimizing taxes on retirement income, including Roth IRA conversions and tax-efficient investing.

i. [Estate Planning]: Discuss the role of estate planning in retirement planning and offer guidance on how to create an effective estate plan.

j. [Financial Advisors]: Offer advice on selecting a financial advisor for retirement planning and discuss the different types of advisors and their areas of expertise.

6. **Tax Planning & Preparation: Offering advice on tax planning and filing.**

    a. [Common Myths]: Identify common myths and misconceptions about tax planning and preparation. Explain how these beliefs can lead to mistakes and offer alternative strategies for effective tax management.

    b. [Maximizing Deductions]: Discuss ways to maximize tax deductions and credits to reduce tax liability. Explain how to identify deductions and credits that apply to specific financial situations and offer tips for effective record-keeping.

    c. [Tax Planning for Retirement]: Discuss how tax planning can play a role in retirement planning. Explain how to choose tax-advantaged retirement accounts and offer advice on how to maximize contributions to these accounts.

    d. [Tax Implications of Investments]: Explain the tax implications of different types of investments, such as stocks, bonds, and real estate. Discuss strategies for tax-efficient investing and offer advice on managing investment gains and losses for tax purposes.

    e. [Filing as a Small Business Owner]: Discuss the unique tax challenges faced by small business owners. Offer advice on record-keeping, tax planning, and filing taxes as a business owner.

f. [Tax Planning for Life Changes]: Discuss how major life changes, such as marriage, divorce, or the birth of a child, can impact tax planning. Offer guidance on how to navigate these changes and optimize tax planning strategies.

g. [Avoiding Tax Scams]: Identify common tax scams and explain how to avoid falling victim to them. Offer tips for verifying the legitimacy of tax preparers and tax-related offers.

h. [State and Local Taxes]: Explain how state and local taxes can impact overall tax liability. Offer guidance on navigating these taxes and identifying strategies to minimize tax liability.

i. [Charitable Giving and Taxes]: Discuss the tax implications of charitable giving and offer advice on how to maximize tax benefits from donations.

j. [Tax Planning for Investment Income]: Explain how investment income is taxed and discuss strategies for managing tax liability associated with investment income. Offer advice on how to balance investment returns with tax consequences.

7. **Insurance: Discussing various types of insurance and helping to determine appropriate coverage.**

a. [Pros and Cons]: Evaluate the advantages and disadvantages of purchasing different types of insurance, such as health, life, or auto insurance. Which types of insurance are necessary and which are optional?

b. [Comparison]: Compare and contrast different

insurance providers and their policies. What are the differences in coverage and pricing between providers?

c. [Risk Assessment]: Discuss the importance of conducting a risk assessment before purchasing insurance. What factors should be considered when determining what type and amount of insurance coverage is needed?

d. [Policy Review]: Analyze common mistakes people make when reviewing their insurance policies. How can individuals ensure they are properly covered and not paying for unnecessary coverage?

e. [Claim Filing]: Explain the process for filing an insurance claim. What information is needed and how can individuals ensure their claim is processed efficiently?

f. [Disaster Preparation]: Discuss the role insurance plays in disaster preparation and recovery. What types of insurance are most important in these situations and how can individuals ensure they are adequately covered?

g. [Budgeting for Insurance]: Offer advice on budgeting for insurance costs. How can individuals incorporate insurance costs into their overall budget and save money on premiums?

h. [Fraud Prevention]: Discuss common insurance scams and how to avoid them. What steps can individuals take to protect themselves from insurance fraud?

i. [Homeowner's Insurance]: Explain the importance of homeowner's insurance and what is typically covered under a homeowner's policy. How can individuals ensure they are properly insured for their home and belongings?

j. [Auto Insurance]: Discuss the different types of auto insurance and what is required in different states. How can individuals ensure they have appropriate coverage for their vehicle?

8. **Homeownership: Providing information on buying, selling, and maintaining a home.**

a. [Pros and Cons]: Discuss the advantages and disadvantages of buying a home versus renting. Offer insights on factors to consider when making this decision.

b. [Costs]: Analyze the true costs of homeownership beyond mortgage payments, such as property taxes, insurance, and maintenance. Offer advice on budgeting for these expenses.

c. [Mortgages]: Discuss different types of mortgages and their pros and cons, including fixed-rate, adjustable-rate, and government-backed options. Offer insights on choosing the right mortgage for individual circumstances.

d. [Home Improvement]: Provide advice on financing and prioritizing home improvement projects, including DIY versus professional work.

  e. [Selling a Home]: Discuss strategies for preparing a home for sale, pricing it effectively, and negotiating offers. Offer insights on working with real estate agents and using online resources.

  f. [Maintenance]: Offer tips for maintaining a home, including seasonal tasks, preventive measures, and identifying and addressing common issues.

  g. [Investment Property]: Discuss the potential benefits and risks of owning an investment property, including rental income and property management responsibilities.

  h. [Home Equity]: Discuss the concept of home equity and how it can be leveraged for other financial goals, such as debt consolidation or funding education.

  i. [Home Insurance]: Discuss the importance of home insurance and the different types of coverage available, such as liability, property damage, and natural disaster protection.

  j. [Real Estate Market]: Analyze trends and forecasts in the real estate market, including factors that can affect home values and opportunities for investment or relocation.

9. **College Savings: Offering guidance on saving for education expenses and understanding financial aid options.**

  a. [Pros and Cons]: Compare and contrast different methods of saving for college, such as 529 plans and Coverdell Education Savings Accounts. Discuss the advantages and disadvantages of each and provide recommendations for parents.

b. [Common Misconceptions]: Identify common misconceptions surrounding financial aid and explain why they are inaccurate. Provide accurate information to help parents make informed decisions about college savings.

c. [Tax Implications]: Discuss the tax implications of different college savings options, including tax-deferred and tax-free options. Offer advice on maximizing tax benefits while saving for college.

d. [Impact of Investments]: Analyze the potential impact of investments on college savings, including risk tolerance, diversification, and expected returns. Offer recommendations for parents on how to balance risk and reward.

e. [Financial Aid Eligibility]: Explain the factors that determine eligibility for financial aid, including income, assets, and family size. Provide strategies for maximizing financial aid while minimizing out-of-pocket expenses.

f. [529 Plan Management]: Discuss the best practices for managing a 529 plan, including choosing the right investment options, monitoring performance, and making contributions. Offer tips for parents to maximize the benefits of their 529 plan.

g. [Scholarship Opportunities]: Explore scholarship opportunities and how they can impact college savings. Provide advice on researching and applying for scholarships to help parents save on college costs.

h. [Starting Early]: Discuss the benefits of starting college savings early and the impact of compound interest on long-term savings. Provide advice on setting savings goals and creating a plan to achieve them.

i. [Using Retirement Accounts]: Discuss the potential benefits and drawbacks of using retirement accounts, such as IRAs and 401(k)s, for college savings. Offer advice on when and how to use retirement accounts for college savings.

j. [Choosing a College]: Discuss the financial considerations that parents should take into account when choosing a college for their child, including the cost of attendance, financial aid opportunities, and post-graduation earning potential. Provide advice on making informed decisions about college selection.

10. **Estate Planning: Discussing wills, trusts, and other aspects of estate planning.**

a. [Benefits of Estate Planning]: Explain the benefits of estate planning and how it can help individuals and families protect their assets and ensure their wishes are carried out.

b. [Estate Planning Myths]: Analyze common misconceptions surrounding estate planning and provide accurate information to help individuals make informed decisions.

c. [Estate Planning for Small Business Owners]: Offer guidance on how small business owners can incorporate their business into their estate plan and ensure a smooth transition for their family or successors.

d. [Digital Assets in Estate Planning]: Discuss the importance of including digital assets in an estate plan and provide tips for identifying and managing these assets.

e. [Estate Planning for Blended Families]: Offer advice on how blended families can navigate the complexities of estate planning and ensure all family members are provided for.

f. [Charitable Giving in Estate Planning]: Explain how charitable giving can be incorporated into an estate plan and provide guidance on selecting the right charitable organization.

g. [Choosing the Right Executor]: Offer advice on how to choose the right executor for an estate and discuss the qualities and responsibilities required for this role.

h. [Estate Planning for High Net Worth Individuals]: Discuss unique considerations for high net worth individuals in estate planning, including tax implications and asset protection strategies.

i. [Estate Planning for Retirement]: Offer guidance on how to plan for retirement through estate planning, including strategies for maximizing retirement savings and minimizing taxes.

j. [Updating an Estate Plan]: Discuss the importance of updating an estate plan periodically and provide guidance on when and how to make changes.

10

Personal Growth Prompts

1. **Goal Setting: Providing guidance on setting and achieving personal and professional goals.**
   a. [SMART Goals]: Discuss the importance of setting specific, measurable, achievable, relevant, and time-bound (SMART) goals when working towards personal or professional objectives. Provide examples of how to apply these principles to goal setting.
   b. [Goal Alignment]: Explore the concept of aligning personal and professional goals to create a fulfilling and purposeful life. Discuss how to identify and prioritize goals that align with one's values and vision for the future.
   c. [Overcoming Obstacles]: Discuss common obstacles that individuals face when trying to achieve their goals, such as lack of motivation or fear of failure. Offer strategies for overcoming

these obstacles and staying on track towards goal attainment.

d. [Visualization Techniques]: Discuss the role of visualization techniques in achieving personal and professional goals. Offer examples of visualization techniques and explain how they can help individuals stay focused and motivated on their goals.

e. [Goal Measurement]: Explore different methods for measuring progress towards personal and professional goals, such as tracking metrics or assessing feedback. Discuss the importance of measuring progress and how it can impact goal attainment.

f. [Accountability]: Discuss the role of accountability in goal setting and achievement. Offer strategies for creating accountability systems, such as finding an accountability partner or joining a support group.

g. [Breaking Down Goals]: Discuss the importance of breaking down large goals into smaller, achievable steps. Offer strategies for breaking down goals and creating action plans to achieve them.

h. [Adjusting Goals]: Explore the concept of adjusting goals as circumstances change or new opportunities arise. Discuss the importance of flexibility in goal setting and offer strategies for adjusting goals while still staying focused and motivated.

i. [Goal Prioritization]: Discuss the importance of prioritizing goals and how to determine which goals should take precedence. Offer strategies for evaluating and prioritizing goals based on factors such as urgency, impact, and alignment with values.

j. [Celebrating Success]: Discuss the importance of celebrating successes and milestones when working towards personal and professional goals. Offer strategies for recognizing and celebrating progress towards goals to maintain motivation and momentum.

2. **Time Management: Offering tips for effectively managing time and increasing productivity.**

a. [Debate]: Discuss the pros and cons of various time management strategies, such as to-do lists, time blocking, and the Pomodoro technique. Explain which strategies may work best for different individuals and situations.

b. [Self-Reflection]: Reflect on your current time management habits and identify areas for improvement. Describe the steps you plan to take to enhance your productivity and efficiency.

c. [Prioritization]: Discuss the importance of prioritizing tasks and provide tips for determining which tasks are most important. Explain how this can lead to more effective time management.

d. [Distraction Management]: Explore common distractions that can derail productivity, such as social media and email notifications. Offer strategies for minimizing or eliminating these distractions.

e. [Goal Alignment]: Explain the importance of aligning goals with values and priorities for effective time management. Discuss how individuals can evaluate their values and priorities to create a more meaningful and productive life.

f. [Procrastination]: Analyze the causes of procrastination and offer tips for overcoming this common obstacle to effective time management. Explain how to break down tasks and make them more manageable.

g. [Time Audit]: Discuss the benefits of conducting a time audit to identify where time is being spent and how it can be better allocated. Offer guidance on how to conduct a time audit and use the results to improve time management.

h. [Accountability]: Explore the benefits of accountability in time management and provide strategies for creating accountability. Explain how this can improve productivity and goal attainment.

i. [Mindfulness]: Discuss the role of mindfulness in time management and offer tips for incorporating mindfulness practices into daily routines. Explain how this can reduce stress and improve productivity.

j. [Work-Life Balance]: Discuss the importance of work-life balance for effective time management and overall well-being. Offer tips for achieving a healthy balance between work, personal life, and leisure time.

3. **Emotional Intelligence: Assisting with the development of emotional awareness and interpersonal skills.**

   a. [Benefits of Emotional Intelligence]: Explain the benefits of developing emotional intelligence and how it can impact personal and professional relationships.

   b. [Emotional Intelligence Assessment]: Discuss various methods for assessing one's level of emotional intelligence and offer guidance on how to improve.

   c. [Emotion Regulation]: Discuss the importance of regulating emotions and provide strategies for managing intense emotions.

   d. [Empathy]: Explain the role of empathy in emotional intelligence and offer tips for improving empathy skills.

   e. [Communication Skills]: Discuss the importance of effective communication in emotional intelligence and offer guidance on developing strong communication skills.

   f. [Conflict Resolution]: Offer strategies for resolving conflicts in a healthy and productive way, utilizing emotional intelligence skills.

   g. [Mindfulness]: Discuss the role of mindfulness

in emotional intelligence and offer techniques for practicing mindfulness.

   h. [Leadership Skills]: Explain how emotional intelligence is related to effective leadership and offer guidance on developing strong leadership skills.

   i. [Cultural Competence]: Discuss the importance of cultural competence in emotional intelligence and offer tips for improving cultural awareness and sensitivity.

   j. [Resilience]: Discuss the role of emotional intelligence in building resilience and offer strategies for developing greater resilience.

4. **Stress Management: Providing strategies for managing and reducing stress.**

   a. [Coping Mechanisms]: Discuss different coping mechanisms that can help in managing stress. Explain how each strategy can be applied and their effectiveness in reducing stress levels.

   b. [Time Management]: Analyze how effective time management can help in reducing stress levels. Discuss different time management techniques and how they can be implemented in daily life.

   c. [Mindfulness]: Explain how mindfulness can help in managing stress. Discuss different mindfulness practices and their effectiveness in reducing stress levels.

   d. [Self-Care]: Discuss the importance of self-care in stress management. Provide tips for incorporating self-care practices into daily routine and explain their effectiveness in reducing stress levels.

e. [Positive Thinking]: Analyze how positive thinking can help in managing stress. Discuss different strategies for positive thinking and how they can be applied in daily life.

f. [Physical Activity]: Explain how physical activity can help in reducing stress levels. Discuss different types of physical activity and their effectiveness in stress management.

g. [Social Support]: Discuss the role of social support in stress management. Explain how to build a support network and the effectiveness of social support in managing stress.

h. [Relaxation Techniques]: Discuss different relaxation techniques that can help in managing stress. Explain how each technique can be applied and their effectiveness in reducing stress levels.

i. [Cognitive Behavioral Therapy]: Explain how cognitive behavioral therapy can help in managing stress. Discuss different techniques used in cognitive behavioral therapy and their effectiveness in stress management.

j. [Work-Life Balance]: Analyze how maintaining a healthy work-life balance can help in managing stress. Provide tips for achieving work-life balance and explain its effectiveness in reducing stress levels.

5. **Communication Skills: Offering guidance on improving verbal and nonverbal communication.**
   a. [Effective Listening]: Discuss the importance of effective listening in communication and provide practical strategies for improving listening skills.
   b. [Nonverbal Communication]: Analyze the role of nonverbal communication in interpersonal interactions and provide tips for improving nonverbal communication.
   c. [Constructive Criticism]: Explain how to give and receive constructive criticism effectively in a professional or personal context.
   d. [Assertiveness]: Discuss the benefits of assertive communication and provide practical tips for being more assertive in interpersonal interactions.
   e. [Conflict Resolution]: Offer guidance on resolving conflicts through effective communication and negotiation techniques.
   f. [Cultural Communication]: Discuss the importance of understanding and respecting cultural differences in communication and provide practical strategies for effective intercultural communication.
   g. [Public Speaking]: Offer guidance on overcoming public speaking anxiety and delivering effective presentations or speeches.
   h. [Written Communication]: Discuss the importance of written communication skills and

provide practical tips for improving written communication in professional or personal contexts.

i. [Active Listening]: Analyze the difference between passive and active listening and provide strategies for becoming a more active listener.

j. [Emotional Intelligence]: Discuss the role of emotional intelligence in effective communication and offer tips for improving emotional awareness and regulation in interpersonal interactions.

6. **Building Confidence: Providing advice on increasing self-confidence and overcoming self-doubt.**

a. [Self-Talk]: Explore the role of self-talk in building confidence. Discuss how positive self-talk can improve self-esteem and provide examples of effective self-talk statements.

b. [Fear of Failure]: Analyze the fear of failure and how it can hinder confidence. Provide strategies for overcoming this fear and building resilience.

c. [Body Language]: Discuss the importance of body language in building confidence. Explain how nonverbal cues can convey confidence and provide tips for improving body language.

d. [Comparisons]: Explore how comparing oneself to others can impact self-confidence. Explain how to shift focus from comparisons to personal growth and self-improvement.

e. [Challenging Beliefs]: Discuss how limiting beliefs can hold us back and impact confidence.

Provide strategies for identifying and challenging these beliefs to build self-confidence.

f. [Acknowledging Strengths]: Discuss the importance of acknowledging personal strengths in building confidence. Provide exercises for identifying and embracing individual strengths.

g. [Setting Goals]: Explore how setting and achieving goals can boost self-confidence. Provide guidance on setting realistic goals and celebrating small wins along the way.

h. [Self-Care]: Discuss the link between self-care and self-confidence. Explain how taking care of oneself physically, emotionally, and mentally can improve confidence levels.

i. [Overcoming Criticism]: Discuss how criticism can impact self-confidence and provide strategies for handling criticism constructively.

j. [Social Support]: Discuss the importance of social support in building confidence. Provide tips for seeking out supportive relationships and building a network of positive influences.

7. **Mindfulness & Meditation: Discussing techniques for cultivating mindfulness and practicing meditation.**

a. [Debate]: Discuss the benefits and drawbacks of mindfulness and meditation for personal growth. Provide examples of how these practices can improve mental health and well-being, and address common misconceptions about their effectiveness.

b. [Comparison]: Compare and contrast different types of meditation and mindfulness techniques, such as focused attention and loving-kindness meditation. Discuss the potential benefits and drawbacks of each approach for personal growth and well-being.

c. [Practical Advice]: Offer practical advice on how to begin a mindfulness or meditation practice, including tips for finding the right technique, establishing a routine, and overcoming common challenges like distraction and restlessness.

d. [Scientific Evidence]: Examine the scientific evidence behind mindfulness and meditation practices, discussing the research on their effectiveness for reducing stress, improving cognitive function, and enhancing emotional well-being. Address common criticisms of the research and offer alternative perspectives.

e. [Cultural Context]: Discuss the cultural and historical origins of mindfulness and meditation practices, examining their roots in Buddhism, Hinduism, and other spiritual traditions. Consider the ways in which these practices have been adapted and incorporated into Western culture.

f. [Self-Awareness]: Discuss how mindfulness and meditation practices can enhance self-awareness and help individuals to better understand their own thoughts, emotions, and behavior patterns. Offer tips for cultivating self-awareness through mindfulness and meditation.

g. [Group Practice]: Discuss the benefits of practicing mindfulness and meditation in a group setting, such as a meditation circle or retreat. Provide tips for finding and participating in a group practice.

h. [Challenges]: Discuss the challenges that individuals may face when attempting to practice mindfulness and meditation, such as feelings of discomfort, difficulty focusing, or resistance to the practice. Offer strategies for overcoming these challenges.

i. [Integration]: Discuss how mindfulness and meditation practices can be integrated into daily life, including tips for incorporating these practices into work, relationships, and other aspects of life. Address common obstacles to integration and offer practical solutions.

j. [Ethical Considerations]: Discuss the ethical considerations surrounding mindfulness and meditation practices, such as issues related to cultural appropriation, power dynamics in teacher-student relationships, and commercialization of the practices. Offer alternative perspectives and considerations for ethical practice.

8. **Healthy Habits: Offering advice on developing and maintaining healthy routines and habits.**

a. [Pros vs Cons]: Analyze the benefits and drawbacks of different healthy habits such as exercising, healthy eating, or getting enough sleep. Explain how these habits can contribute to overall well-being and offer tips for establishing and maintaining healthy habits.

b. [Myth Busting]: Analyze common misconceptions surrounding healthy habits and explain how they can be harmful or ineffective. Offer alternative strategies for developing healthy habits.

c. [Personalization]: Discuss the importance of personalizing healthy habits to fit individual needs and lifestyles. Provide examples of how different individuals may need to modify their habits and offer tips for finding what works best for each person.

d. [Behavioral Change]: Analyze the stages of behavior change and explain how to apply them to developing and maintaining healthy habits. Offer practical tips for each stage of the process.

e. [Accountability]: Discuss the importance of accountability in developing and maintaining healthy habits. Offer strategies for finding accountability partners or setting up systems to hold oneself accountable.

f. [Time Management]: Discuss how time management is important for developing and maintaining healthy habits. Offer tips for prioritizing healthy habits and making time for them in a busy schedule.

g. [Small Changes]: Discuss how small changes can add up to make a big difference in developing healthy habits. Offer tips for identifying small changes that can be made and implementing them gradually over time.

h. [Mindful Eating]: Discuss the importance of mindful eating in developing healthy eating habits. Offer tips for practicing mindful eating and avoiding mindless eating habits.

i. [Self-Care]: Discuss how self-care is an essential part of maintaining healthy habits. Offer tips for identifying self-care practices that work for each individual and incorporating them into daily routines.

j. [Social Support]: Discuss the importance of social support in developing and maintaining healthy habits. Offer tips for building a support system and seeking out positive social influences.

9. **Work-Life Balance: Providing guidance on achieving a balance between personal and professional responsibilities.**

a. [Pros and Cons]: Discuss the pros and cons of different work-life balance strategies. Evaluate how these strategies affect personal and professional well-being.

b. [Myths and Reality]: Analyze common myths and misconceptions about work-life balance.

Provide evidence-based information to debunk these myths and offer practical tips for achieving a better balance.

c. [Boundaries]: Discuss the importance of setting boundaries between work and personal life. Offer practical advice for maintaining these boundaries and creating a healthy balance.

d. [Coping with Overwhelm]: Analyze common challenges that individuals face when trying to balance work and personal responsibilities. Provide strategies for coping with overwhelm and achieving a better balance.

e. [Productivity vs. Self-Care]: Discuss the tension between productivity and self-care in achieving work-life balance. Evaluate the benefits and drawbacks of prioritizing one over the other and offer strategies for balancing both.

f. [Flexible Work Arrangements]: Evaluate the effectiveness of flexible work arrangements in achieving work-life balance. Discuss common challenges and offer advice for navigating these arrangements.

g. [Changing Priorities]: Discuss how priorities may shift over time in achieving work-life balance. Provide strategies for adapting to these changes and maintaining a healthy balance.

h. [Family Dynamics]: Analyze how family dynamics can affect work-life balance. Provide advice for navigating these dynamics and maintaining a healthy balance.

   i. [Mindset Shift]: Discuss how a mindset shift can help individuals achieve a better work-life balance. Provide strategies for changing mindset and overcoming common obstacles.

   j. [Self-Reflection]: Encourage self-reflection on personal values and goals in achieving work-life balance. Provide guidance on setting achievable goals and developing a plan to achieve them.

10. **Resilience & Adaptability: Assisting with building resilience and adapting to change and challenges.**

   a. [Benefits of Resilience]: Discuss the benefits of developing resilience and how it can lead to personal growth and success in various areas of life.

   b. [Adapting to Change]: Offer tips on how to adapt to change in personal and professional situations and the importance of being adaptable in a rapidly changing world.

   c. [Overcoming Adversity]: Share personal stories of overcoming adversity and offer advice on how to build resilience and overcome challenges in life.

   d. [Mindset Shift]: Discuss the importance of mindset in building resilience and offer strategies for shifting to a growth mindset in the face of challenges.

   e. [Handling Stressful Situations]: Offer guidance

on how to handle stressful situations and build resilience through effective coping mechanisms.

f. [Resilience in the Workplace]: Discuss how resilience can lead to success in the workplace and offer strategies for building resilience in a professional setting.

g. [Embracing Failure]: Discuss the importance of failure in building resilience and offer advice on how to reframe failure as a learning opportunity.

h. [Building Emotional Strength]: Offer tips on how to build emotional strength and resilience through self-care and mental health practices.

i. [Developing Problem-Solving Skills]: Discuss how developing problem-solving skills can lead to greater resilience and offer strategies for improving problem-solving abilities.

j. [Managing Change]: Offer guidance on how to manage change effectively and build resilience through adaptability and a growth mindset.

11

Persuasion & Influence Prompts

1. **Building Rapport: Offering techniques for establishing trust and rapport with others.**
   a. [Active Listening]: Discuss the importance of active listening in building rapport with others. Provide examples of active listening techniques and explain how they can help establish trust and understanding.
   b. [Body Language]: Explore the role of body language in building rapport with others. Explain how nonverbal cues such as eye contact, posture, and facial expressions can convey trust and openness.
   c. [Empathy]: Discuss the role of empathy in building rapport with others. Explain how the ability to understand and share the feelings of others can help establish a deeper connection.

d. [Common Ground]: Analyze the importance of finding common ground when building rapport with others. Provide examples of how to identify shared interests or values and how they can be used to establish trust and understanding.

e. [Mirroring]: Explain the technique of mirroring and its role in building rapport with others. Provide examples of how to mirror body language, tone of voice, and other nonverbal cues to establish a connection.

f. [Authenticity]: Discuss the importance of authenticity in building rapport with others. Explain how being genuine and transparent can help establish trust and credibility.

g. [Personal Branding]: Explore the role of personal branding in building rapport with others. Discuss how a strong personal brand can help establish trust and credibility.

h. [Networking]: Discuss the role of networking in building rapport with others. Provide tips on how to effectively network and establish meaningful connections with others.

i. [Positive Attitude]: Analyze the role of a positive attitude in building rapport with others. Explain how maintaining a positive outlook can help establish trust and create a welcoming environment.

j. [Adapting Communication Style]: Explain how adapting one's communication style can help build rapport with others. Provide examples of how to adjust one's tone, language, and style to better connect with different individuals.

2. **Effective Communication: Providing guidance on expressing ideas clearly and persuasively.**
   a. [Persuasive Techniques]: Discuss different persuasive techniques, such as using emotional appeals or logic, and how to use them effectively to communicate your ideas.
   b. [Active Listening]: Explain the importance of active listening in effective communication and provide tips for improving this skill.
   c. [Body Language]: Discuss the role of body language in communication and provide tips for using it effectively to convey your message.
   d. [Language Choice]: Analyze the impact of language choice in communication, such as using positive versus negative language, and provide tips for using language effectively.
   e. [Storytelling]: Explain how storytelling can be a powerful tool for persuasion and offer tips for crafting compelling stories to communicate your ideas.
   f. [Building Credibility]: Discuss the importance of building credibility in communication and offer tips for establishing yourself as a trustworthy and reliable source.
   g. [Persuasion Ethics]: Analyze the ethical considerations of persuasion and influence and discuss

strategies for using these skills in an ethical and responsible manner.

   h. [Audience Analysis]: Explain the importance of understanding your audience in communication and offer tips for analyzing your audience to tailor your message effectively.

   i. [Power Dynamics]: Discuss the role of power dynamics in communication and offer strategies for navigating power imbalances to achieve effective communication.

   j. [Persuasion and Conflict Resolution]: Explain how persuasion and influence can be used to resolve conflicts and offer tips for using these skills in conflict resolution scenarios.

3. **Storytelling: Discussing the art of storytelling as a tool for persuasion.**

   a. [Personal Connection]: Describe a time when a story was used to persuade you. Explain how the story made you feel and whether it influenced your decision.

   b. [Power of Narrative]: Discuss the power of storytelling in influencing public opinion on social and political issues. Provide examples of successful and unsuccessful attempts to use storytelling for persuasion.

   c. [Emotional Appeal]: Analyze the use of emotional appeal in storytelling for persuasion. Discuss the potential ethical concerns and the importance of balancing emotions with logic.

d. [Cultural Significance]: Explore the cultural significance of storytelling in different regions of the world. Explain how cultural values and beliefs influence the use of storytelling for persuasion.

e. [Elements of Storytelling]: Identify and explain the key elements of effective storytelling for persuasion. Discuss how each element contributes to the persuasive power of a story.

f. [Visual Storytelling]: Discuss the use of visual storytelling for persuasion. Provide examples of effective visual storytelling and explain how visuals can enhance the persuasive impact of a story.

g. [Storytelling and Branding]: Analyze the role of storytelling in branding and marketing. Discuss how brands use storytelling to connect with consumers and build brand loyalty.

h. [Storytelling in Leadership]: Discuss the importance of storytelling in effective leadership. Provide examples of leaders who have successfully used storytelling to inspire and persuade others.

i. [Authenticity in Storytelling]: Analyze the importance of authenticity in storytelling for persuasion. Discuss the potential risks of using inauthentic stories and how to ensure the authenticity of a story.

j. [Storytelling in Conflict Resolution]: Discuss the use of storytelling in conflict resolution. Explain how stories can help bridge divides and build understanding between conflicting parties.

4. **Active Listening: Offering advice on developing active listening skills for better understanding and influence.**

    a. [Reflective Listening]: Describe the benefits of reflective listening and provide techniques for developing this skill to enhance communication and persuasion in various settings.

    b. [Empathetic Listening]: Discuss the importance of empathetic listening and how it can be used to build rapport and influence others in personal and professional contexts.

    c. [Body Language]: Analyze the role of body language in active listening and communication, and offer tips for improving body language to increase persuasive impact.

    d. [Questioning Techniques]: Explain how questioning techniques can be used to promote active listening and understanding, and offer examples of effective questioning strategies for different contexts.

    e. [Nonverbal Communication]: Discuss the impact of nonverbal communication on persuasion and influence, and provide advice on developing awareness and control of nonverbal cues.

    f. [Communication Styles]: Explore different communication styles and how they can be adapted to match the preferences of different individuals and groups, in order to increase persuasive power.

g. [Credibility]: Analyze the importance of credibility in persuasion and influence, and provide advice on building and maintaining credibility through communication and behavior.

h. [Persuasive Language]: Offer guidance on using persuasive language to increase the impact of communication, including techniques such as emotional appeals and framing.

i. [Active Listening in Conflict Resolution]: Describe how active listening can be used as a tool for conflict resolution, and provide strategies for applying this approach effectively.

j. [Cultural Differences]: Discuss the impact of cultural differences on communication and persuasion, and provide advice on how to navigate these differences in order to increase persuasive impact.

5. **Nonverbal Communication: Providing tips on using body language and facial expressions to enhance persuasion.**

a. [Nonverbal Persuasion]: Analyze the different types of nonverbal communication and explain how each can be used to influence others. Provide examples of how to utilize these techniques effectively in real-life situations.

b. [Facial Expressions]: Discuss the impact of facial expressions on persuasion and provide tips for how to use them effectively in different contexts.

Offer examples of when to use different facial expressions for maximum impact.

c. [Body Language]: Analyze the different types of body language and explain how they can be used to convey persuasive messages. Provide examples of how to use body language to enhance communication and influence others.

d. [Tone of Voice]: Discuss the importance of tone of voice in persuasion and provide tips for using it effectively. Offer examples of how to use tone of voice to convey different emotions and influence others.

e. [Eye Contact]: Analyze the role of eye contact in nonverbal communication and persuasion. Provide tips for how to use eye contact effectively to convey confidence and build rapport with others.

f. [Personal Space]: Discuss the impact of personal space on nonverbal communication and persuasion. Offer tips for how to use personal space effectively to convey power and influence in different situations.

g. [Mirroring]: Explain the concept of mirroring in nonverbal communication and persuasion. Provide examples of how to use mirroring effectively to build rapport and establish trust with others.

h. [Gestures]: Analyze the different types of gestures and explain how they can be used to convey persuasive messages. Provide examples of how to use gestures to enhance communication and influence others.

i. [Cultural Differences]: Discuss the impact of cultural differences on nonverbal communication and persuasion. Offer tips for how to navigate cultural differences in nonverbal communication to convey messages effectively.

j. [Authenticity]: Explain the importance of authenticity in nonverbal communication and persuasion. Provide tips for how to be authentic while using nonverbal techniques to influence others.

6. **Emotional Appeals: Discussing the role of emotions in persuasion and how to use them effectively.**

a. [Appealing to Emotions]: Discuss the importance of emotional appeals in persuasive communication. Explain how they can be used effectively to influence others and provide examples of situations where emotional appeals may be appropriate or inappropriate.

b. [Emotional Intelligence]: Discuss the role of emotional intelligence in persuasive communication. Explain how understanding one's own emotions and those of others can be used to enhance the effectiveness of emotional appeals.

c. [Empathy]: Discuss the importance of empathy in persuasive communication. Explain how empathy can be used to build rapport and establish trust with others, and provide examples of situations where empathy may be particularly effective.

d. [The Power of Storytelling]: Discuss how storytelling can be used to make emotional appeals in persuasive communication. Explain how stories can be used to evoke emotions and influence others, and provide examples of effective storytelling in persuasive communication.

e. [The Ethics of Emotional Appeals]: Analyze the ethical implications of using emotional appeals in persuasive communication. Explain how emotional appeals can be used to manipulate or exploit others, and provide guidance on how to use emotional appeals ethically.

f. [Neuroscience and Persuasion]: Discuss the neuroscience behind emotional appeals in persuasive communication. Explain how understanding the brain's response to emotional appeals can be used to enhance the effectiveness of persuasion.

g. [Nonverbal Cues]: Discuss the role of nonverbal cues in emotional appeals and persuasion. Explain how body language, facial expressions, and tone of voice can be used to convey emotions and influence others.

h. [Targeted Emotional Appeals]: Discuss how emotional appeals can be tailored to different audiences and demographics. Explain how understanding the emotional triggers of specific groups can be used to create more effective emotional appeals.

   i. [The Power of Positive Emotions]: Discuss the role of positive emotions in persuasive communication. Explain how positive emotions can be used to create a more favorable attitude towards a message or idea, and provide examples of effective use of positive emotions in persuasive communication.

   j. [Dealing with Emotional Resistance]: Discuss strategies for dealing with emotional resistance in persuasive communication. Explain how to handle negative emotions such as anger, fear, or skepticism, and provide guidance on how to turn emotional resistance into a positive response.

7. **Logical Argumentation: Offering guidance on constructing logical and compelling arguments.**

   a. [Logical Fallacies]: Identify and explain common logical fallacies and how they can weaken an argument. Offer strategies to avoid or overcome these fallacies.

   b. [Evidence-Based Argumentation]: Discuss the importance of using evidence to support arguments and provide guidance on how to find and use credible sources of information.

   c. [Counterarguments]: Explain the role of counterarguments in building a strong argument and offer tips on how to anticipate and address potential objections.

d. [Persuasive Language]: Discuss the impact of persuasive language on effective argumentation and offer techniques for using language to enhance persuasiveness.

e. [Argument Structure]: Provide guidance on structuring arguments effectively, including the use of claims, evidence, and warrants.

f. [Value-Based Argumentation]: Discuss the use of values and ethical considerations in persuasive argumentation, including how to appeal to shared values and address ethical concerns.

g. [Logical Reasoning]: Discuss the importance of logical reasoning in effective argumentation and provide guidance on developing strong reasoning skills.

h. [Emotional Appeal]: Discuss the role of emotional appeal in argumentation and provide guidance on how to use emotional appeal effectively without sacrificing logic and credibility.

i. [Audience Analysis]: Explain the importance of audience analysis in persuasive argumentation and provide guidance on how to tailor arguments to specific audiences.

j. [Rebuttal and Refutation]: Discuss the importance of rebuttal and refutation in effective argumentation and provide guidance on how to effectively respond to opposing arguments.

8. **Framing & Reframing: Providing techniques for**

presenting information in a way that influences perceptions.

a. [Framing]: Discuss the concept of framing in persuasion and provide examples of how it can be used to influence perceptions.

b. [Reframing]: Explain the technique of reframing in persuasion and offer strategies for effectively reframing information to change perceptions.

c. [Framing vs. Reframing]: Compare and contrast the differences between framing and reframing in persuasion, and discuss when each technique is most effective.

d. [Emotional Framing]: Discuss the use of emotions in framing messages and offer techniques for using emotional appeals to influence perceptions.

e. [Cognitive Framing]: Analyze the role of cognitive framing in persuasion and provide examples of how it can be used to influence perceptions.

f. [Framing Bias]: Discuss the potential for framing bias in persuasive communication and offer strategies for avoiding or minimizing its effects.

g. [Value Framing]: Explain the concept of value framing in persuasion and offer techniques for using it to influence perceptions and behaviors.

h. [Framing Effects]: Analyze the different framing effects that can impact persuasion, such as the framing effect, priming effect, and anchoring effect, and provide strategies for minimizing their negative impact.

    i. [Framing and Culture]: Discuss how cultural differences can impact framing and reframing in persuasion and offer techniques for effectively communicating across cultures.

    j. [Ethics of Framing]: Analyze the ethical considerations involved in using framing and reframing techniques in persuasion and discuss the potential risks and benefits of these strategies.

9. **Overcoming Objections: Discussing strategies for addressing and overcoming objections during persuasion.**

    a. [Common Objections]: Identify and analyze common objections that arise during the persuasion process. Offer effective strategies for addressing and overcoming these objections.

    b. [Empathy]: Discuss the role of empathy in overcoming objections during persuasion. Offer techniques for demonstrating empathy and building rapport with the person being persuaded.

    c. [Anticipating Objections]: Explain the importance of anticipating objections during the persuasion process. Provide strategies for anticipating objections and preparing responses.

    d. [Framing Objections]: Discuss the power of framing objections in a positive light during the persuasion process. Offer techniques for reframing objections and turning them into opportunities for persuasion.

e. [Active Listening]: Explain the importance of active listening when addressing objections during the persuasion process. Offer strategies for active listening and responding to objections.

f. [Handling Rejection]: Discuss techniques for handling rejection during the persuasion process. Offer strategies for remaining calm and professional in the face of rejection.

g. [Problem Solving]: Explain how problem-solving can be an effective strategy for overcoming objections during the persuasion process. Offer techniques for identifying solutions to objections and presenting them in a persuasive manner.

h. [Stress Reduction]: Discuss the importance of stress reduction when addressing objections during the persuasion process. Offer techniques for reducing stress and remaining calm under pressure.

i. [Building Trust]: Discuss the role of trust in the persuasion process and offer techniques for building trust with the person being persuaded.

j. [Perseverance]: Explain the importance of perseverance in the face of objections during the persuasion process. Offer strategies for maintaining focus and staying motivated despite setbacks.

10. **Ethical Persuasion: Offering advice on using persuasion ethically and responsibly.**

a. [Moral Dilemma]: Discuss the ethical considerations involved in using persuasion. Describe a situation where persuasion may cross ethical boundaries and offer alternative approaches that align with ethical principles.

b. [Impact Analysis]: Analyze the potential impact of using unethical persuasion tactics on the individual, society, and the environment. Offer ways to mitigate negative effects and promote ethical persuasion.

c. [Debate]: Debate the pros and cons of using ethical persuasion in marketing and advertising. Argue for or against the use of ethical persuasion in these contexts and provide evidence to support your position.

d. [Real-Life Examples]: Examine real-life examples of ethical and unethical persuasion in politics, business, or personal relationships. Discuss the impact of these examples and how they can inform our own use of persuasion.

e. [Responsibility]: Discuss the responsibility that comes with the power of persuasion. Explain how individuals can use persuasion ethically and responsibly, and what measures can be taken to prevent misuse.

f. [Values Alignment]: Offer advice on how to align persuasive messages with the values of the audience to increase the effectiveness and ethicality of persuasion. Provide examples of how this approach can be applied in different contexts.

g. [Trust Building]: Discuss how building trust with the audience is a crucial aspect of ethical persuasion. Offer techniques for building trust, such as transparency, authenticity, and empathy.

h. [Cultural Considerations]: Analyze how cultural differences can impact ethical persuasion. Discuss cultural norms and values that should be taken into consideration when using persuasion in different contexts and how to navigate cultural differences.

i. [Self-Reflection]: Encourage self-reflection on personal values and beliefs related to ethical persuasion. Offer exercises or questions to help individuals assess their own values and how they inform their use of persuasion.

j. [Regulation]: Discuss the role of regulation in promoting ethical persuasion. Analyze existing regulations in different industries and offer suggestions for improving or implementing regulation to ensure ethical use of persuasion.

Social Media Management Prompts

1. **Content Creation and Curation: Offering guidance on creating and curating engaging social media content that resonates with the target audience.**

   a. [Social Media Goals]: Discuss the importance of setting clear social media goals and objectives for effective content creation and curation. Provide examples of how different goals can influence the type of content created and curated.

   b. [Target Audience]: Analyze the target audience and identify their preferences, interests, and pain points to create and curate social media content that resonates with them. Provide tips on conducting audience research and adapting content to different social media platforms.

   c. [Content Strategy]: Develop a social media content strategy that aligns with the brand's goals and the target audience's needs. Discuss different content types, themes, and formats and how to balance promotional and educational content.

d. [Trending Topics]: Discuss the importance of staying up-to-date with trending topics and incorporating them into social media content to increase engagement and reach. Provide tips on identifying relevant trends and adapting them to the brand's voice and values.

e. [Visual Content]: Emphasize the importance of visual content in social media and provide tips on creating and curating eye-catching graphics, videos, and photos. Discuss the role of branding and consistency in visual content creation.

f. [Content Calendar]: Develop a content calendar to plan and organize social media content in advance. Discuss the benefits of having a content calendar and provide tips on creating one that aligns with the brand's goals and target audience's needs.

g. [User-Generated Content]: Discuss the benefits of user-generated content and provide tips on encouraging and curating it. Discuss the role of authenticity and trust in user-generated content and how it can boost engagement and brand loyalty.

h. [Content Optimization]: Discuss techniques for optimizing social media content, such as using hashtags, optimizing captions, and leveraging analytics. Provide tips on measuring and analyzing social media metrics to improve content creation and curation.

i. [Social Media Tools]: Introduce different social media tools and software that can help streamline content creation and curation. Discuss the benefits and drawbacks of each tool and how to choose the right ones for the brand's goals and target audience's needs.

j. [Content Testing]: Discuss the importance of testing and experimenting with social media content to identify what works and what doesn't. Provide tips on A/B testing, split testing, and analyzing metrics to refine content creation and curation.

2. **Social Media Strategy and Planning: Sharing tips for developing and implementing comprehensive social media strategies and editorial calendars.**

   a. [Audience Analysis]: Explain the importance of audience analysis in developing a social media strategy and planning editorial calendars. Discuss different techniques for understanding the target audience's preferences, interests, and behaviors.

   b. [Content Planning]: Discuss the role of content planning in developing a comprehensive social media strategy. Provide tips for identifying relevant themes and topics and creating a content calendar that aligns with the brand's objectives.

   c. [Competitor Analysis]: Explore the importance

of conducting competitor analysis to inform social media strategy and planning. Discuss techniques for identifying and evaluating competitor content and engagement strategies.

d. [Platform Selection]: Explain the importance of selecting the right social media platforms for a brand's social media strategy. Discuss the pros and cons of different platforms and how to choose the best fit for a brand's target audience and objectives.

e. [Engagement Strategies]: Provide guidance on developing engagement strategies that drive audience interaction and increase social media engagement. Discuss the importance of responding to comments and messages and creating opportunities for user-generated content.

f. [Measurement and Analytics]: Discuss the importance of measuring social media performance and using analytics to inform social media strategy and planning. Provide guidance on setting KPIs and tracking metrics to evaluate content effectiveness and adjust strategies accordingly.

g. [Budgeting]: Explore the importance of budgeting for social media management and advertising. Discuss different advertising options on social media platforms and provide guidance on how to allocate budget effectively.

h. [Crisis Management]: Discuss the importance of having a crisis management plan in place for social media. Provide guidance on responding to negative comments and reviews and managing a social media crisis.

i. [Influencer Marketing]: Discuss the benefits and drawbacks of influencer marketing in a social media strategy. Provide guidance on identifying and selecting the right influencers and developing effective collaborations.

j. [Social Media Policy]: Explain the importance of having a clear social media policy for employees and stakeholders. Provide guidance on developing a policy that outlines expectations and guidelines for social media use.

3. **Social Media Analytics and Reporting: Providing advice on tracking, measuring, and analyzing social media performance using key metrics and reporting tools.**

a. [Social Media Metrics]: Discuss the key social media metrics that businesses should track and measure, such as engagement rates, reach, and conversion rates. Provide examples of how to use these metrics to optimize social media content and strategy.

b. [Reporting Tools]: Introduce social media reporting tools and dashboards that can help businesses track and analyze their social media performance more efficiently. Provide tips for selecting and using the right reporting tools for different business needs.

c. [Competitive Analysis]: Discuss the importance of conducting competitive analysis on social media platforms to gain insights into industry trends and best practices. Provide examples of tools and techniques for conducting effective competitive analysis.

d. [Social Media Advertising]: Discuss the benefits and drawbacks of social media advertising and provide tips for creating effective ad campaigns on different social media platforms.

e. [Social Media Listening]: Introduce the concept of social media listening and explain how it can be used to monitor brand reputation, gather customer feedback, and identify emerging trends in the industry.

f. [Influencer Marketing]: Discuss the role of influencer marketing in social media strategy and provide tips for identifying and partnering with relevant influencers to promote brand awareness and engagement.

g. [Community Building]: Discuss the importance of community building on social media and provide tips for engaging with followers and fostering a sense of community around the brand.

h. [Content Calendar]: Introduce the concept of a social media content calendar and explain how it can be used to plan and organize social media content more effectively. Provide tips for creating and implementing a successful content calendar.

i. [Brand Voice and Tone]: Discuss the importance of developing a consistent brand voice and tone on social media and provide tips for maintaining a cohesive and authentic brand image across all social media channels.

j. [Social Media Crisis Management]: Discuss the importance of having a crisis management plan in place for social media and provide tips for managing and responding to negative feedback or crises on social media

4. **Social Media Advertising: Exploring best practices for creating and managing paid social media campaigns, including targeting, budgeting, and ad creatives.**

   a. [Social Media Platforms]: Analyze the strengths and weaknesses of different social media platforms for advertising, such as Facebook, Instagram, Twitter, and LinkedIn. Discuss how to choose the most appropriate platform based on the target audience and advertising goals.

   b. [Ad Targeting]: Discuss the importance of effective ad targeting in social media advertising and the various options available, such as demographic targeting, interest targeting, and location targeting. Provide tips for optimizing ad targeting for maximum ROI.

   c. [Ad Creatives]: Explore best practices for creating compelling ad creatives for social media advertising, such as using eye-catching visuals, clear messaging, and strong calls-to-action. Discuss how to tailor ad creatives to specific platforms and target audiences.

d. [Budgeting]: Provide guidance on setting and managing social media advertising budgets, including strategies for optimizing spend and measuring ROI. Discuss how to adjust budgets based on campaign performance and changing business needs.

e. [Ad Management]: Discuss effective strategies for managing and monitoring social media ad campaigns, including scheduling, bidding, and monitoring performance metrics. Provide tips for troubleshooting and optimizing campaigns for better results.

f. [Retargeting]: Explain the concept of retargeting in social media advertising and how it can be used to re-engage potential customers who have interacted with previous ads or visited a website. Provide examples of successful retargeting campaigns.

g. [Ad Policies and Guidelines]: Discuss the various policies and guidelines set by social media platforms for advertising, such as prohibited content and ad formats. Explain how to ensure compliance with these policies while still creating effective ad campaigns.

h. [Influencer Marketing]: Explore the concept of influencer marketing and how it can be used in social media advertising. Discuss best practices for identifying and working with influencers, as well as measuring the success of influencer campaigns.

i. [Ad Testing and Optimization]: Provide guidance on testing and optimizing social media ad campaigns to improve performance and ROI. Discuss various testing methods, such as A/B testing and multivariate testing, and how to interpret and act on the results.

j. [Ad Reporting]: Discuss the importance of regular ad reporting for tracking campaign performance and identifying areas for improvement. Provide tips for creating effective ad reports and presenting the results to stakeholders.

5. **Social Media Platforms: Discussing the features, benefits, and unique challenges of various social media platforms, such as Facebook, Instagram, Twitter, and LinkedIn.**

a. [Platform Selection]: Compare and contrast the different social media platforms, such as Facebook, Twitter, and Instagram, in terms of their target audience, content format, and engagement strategies. Provide recommendations for which platforms are best suited for different business goals and objectives.

b. [Content Planning]: Discuss the process of planning and creating social media content that resonates with the target audience and aligns with brand messaging. Provide examples of effective content strategies and how they can be adapted to different social media platforms.

c. [Hashtag Strategies]: Explore the use of hashtags in social media marketing and discuss effective hashtag strategies for increasing visibility and engagement. Provide examples of successful hashtag campaigns and how they were executed.

d. [Influencer Marketing]: Discuss the use of influencer marketing in social media, including the benefits, challenges, and best practices for working with influencers to promote brands and products.

e. [Community Building]: Explore strategies for building and engaging a social media community, including tactics for responding to customer inquiries and comments, creating user-generated content, and fostering brand advocacy.

f. [Social Media Listening]: Discuss the importance of social media listening for monitoring brand reputation, identifying customer needs and preferences, and tracking industry trends. Provide examples of effective social media listening strategies and tools.

g. [Performance Metrics]: Explore the different social media metrics, such as engagement rate, reach, and conversions, and their significance in evaluating social media performance. Discuss best practices for measuring and analyzing social media data to inform content and advertising strategies.

h. [Brand Persona]: Discuss the development of a brand persona for social media, including the importance of consistency, authenticity, and tone in messaging. Provide examples of successful brand personas and how they have contributed to social media success.

i. [Social Media Crisis Management]: Discuss effective strategies for managing social media crises, including steps for identifying and responding to negative feedback and developing a crisis communication plan.

j. [Social Media Policy]: Explore the importance of establishing social media policies and guidelines for employees, including best practices for protecting brand reputation and ensuring compliance with legal and ethical standards.

6. **Community Management and Engagement: Offering strategies for fostering and maintaining a positive, engaged online community on social media platforms.**

   a. [Community Building]: Discuss the key elements of building a strong online community on social media, including consistent engagement, active listening, and fostering two-way conversations.

   b. [User-Generated Content]: Explore the benefits and challenges of incorporating user-generated content into social media strategies, and provide tips for encouraging and promoting user participation.

  c. [Responding to Feedback]: Discuss the importance of responding to feedback and criticism on social media, and provide best practices for addressing negative comments and reviews.

  d. [Influencer Marketing]: Analyze the role of influencer marketing in social media management, and provide tips for identifying and partnering with influencers to promote brand awareness and engagement.

  e. [Brand Voice]: Discuss the importance of establishing and maintaining a consistent brand voice across social media platforms, and provide examples of how to adapt brand messaging to different audiences and channels.

  f. [Social Listening]: Explain the concept of social listening and its importance in community management and engagement on social media, and provide tips for using social listening tools and techniques effectively.

  g. [Customer Service]: Discuss the role of social media in customer service and support, and provide best practices for responding to customer inquiries and issues on social media platforms.

  h. [Crises Management]: Explore strategies for managing social media crises, including responding quickly and transparently, apologizing when necessary, and providing solutions or alternatives.

    i. [Engagement Metrics]: Discuss key engagement metrics on social media platforms, such as likes, shares, and comments, and provide tips for measuring and analyzing engagement data to optimize social media strategies.

    j. [Collaboration]: Discuss the benefits of collaboration and partnerships in social media management, and provide examples of successful collaborations and tips for initiating and maintaining partnerships with other businesses and influencers.

7. **Social Media Automation and Scheduling: Recommending tools and techniques for automating and scheduling social media content to improve efficiency and consistency.**

    a. [Content Curation]: Discuss the benefits and drawbacks of using social media automation and scheduling tools for content curation. Provide examples of effective strategies and best practices for scheduling content to maximize engagement.

    b. [Social Media Management Tools]: Analyze different social media management tools and their features for automating and scheduling content. Discuss their strengths and weaknesses and provide recommendations for selecting the best tool based on business needs and goals.

    c. [Consistency in Posting]: Discuss the importance of consistency in social media posting for building brand awareness and engagement. Provide tips and techniques for scheduling and automating social media content to maintain a consistent posting schedule.

d. [Personalization]: Discuss how to balance automation and personalization in social media content creation and curation. Provide examples of effective personalization techniques for increasing engagement while still maintaining consistency.

e. [Engagement Metrics]: Discuss the importance of tracking engagement metrics, such as likes, shares, and comments, for measuring the effectiveness of social media automation and scheduling. Provide tips for tracking and analyzing these metrics and adjusting strategies accordingly.

f. [Audience Segmentation]: Discuss the benefits of audience segmentation for effective social media automation and scheduling. Provide tips for segmenting audiences based on demographics, interests, and behaviors to create targeted content and increase engagement.

g. [Content Planning]: Discuss the importance of content planning and how it can help with social media automation and scheduling. Provide tips for creating a content plan and aligning it with business goals and target audience.

h. [Timing]: Discuss the importance of timing in social media automation and scheduling. Provide tips for determining the best times to post content based on audience behavior and engagement metrics.

    i. [Customization]: Discuss the benefits of customization in social media automation and scheduling, such as tailoring content to specific social media platforms and target audiences. Provide examples of effective customization techniques and how they can be implemented using social media management tools.

    j. [Data Analytics]: Discuss how data analytics can be used to optimize social media automation and scheduling strategies. Provide tips for collecting and analyzing data, identifying trends and patterns, and using them to improve social media performance.

8. **Influencer Marketing: Providing guidance on collaborating with influencers and leveraging their reach and influence for brand promotion.**

    a. [Influencer Identification]: Discuss effective ways to identify potential influencers for collaborations, such as analyzing their engagement rates, niche relevance, and audience demographics. Provide examples of successful influencer campaigns and how they align with brand objectives.

    b. [Influencer Outreach]: Provide tips and best practices for reaching out to influencers and building successful partnerships, including personalized outreach, offering unique incentives, and fostering authentic relationships.

c. [Influencer Contracting]: Discuss the legal and financial aspects of influencer marketing, such as drafting contracts, negotiating rates, and ensuring compliance with FTC regulations.

d. [Influencer Content Creation]: Offer advice on creating effective and authentic sponsored content with influencers that resonates with both the brand and the influencer's audience.

e. [Influencer Performance Measurement]: Discuss methods for measuring the success of influencer marketing campaigns, such as tracking engagement rates, conversions, and brand sentiment. Provide examples of key metrics to monitor and tools to use for tracking performance.

f. [Micro-Influencers]: Explore the benefits of working with micro-influencers, including their high engagement rates, niche relevance, and lower cost. Provide examples of successful micro-influencer campaigns and how they differ from traditional influencer collaborations.

g. [Influencer Marketing Mistakes]: Discuss common mistakes brands make when working with influencers, such as lack of research, mismatched partnerships, and inauthentic content. Provide tips for avoiding these pitfalls.

h. [Influencer and Brand Alignment]: Discuss the importance of finding influencers that align with the brand's values and objectives, and offer strategies for identifying the right fit.

i. [Influencer Campaign Planning]: Provide advice on creating a comprehensive influencer marketing plan, including setting goals, identifying target audiences, and developing a content strategy.

j. [Influencer Marketing Trends]: Explore the latest trends and innovations in influencer marketing, such as the rise of video content, the importance of long-term partnerships, and the use of AI and machine learning for influencer discovery and measurement.

9. **Social Listening and Reputation Management: Sharing tips for monitoring and managing brand sentiment and reputation on social media platforms.**

a. [Brand Perception]: Explain how social listening can help businesses understand their brand perception and reputation on social media platforms. Discuss the importance of monitoring social media mentions, reviews, and comments, and provide strategies for responding to negative feedback.

b. [Social Media Monitoring]: Discuss different social media monitoring tools and their features. Explain how businesses can use these tools to track their brand mentions, industry trends, and competitors, and provide examples of successful implementation.

c. [Reputation Management]: Discuss the importance of reputation management on social media platforms and its impact on businesses. Provide strategies for addressing negative reviews, comments, and feedback, and share examples of successful reputation management.

d. [Social Media Crisis Management]: Discuss how businesses can prepare for and handle social media crises, such as negative reviews or viral social media incidents. Provide examples of successful crisis management strategies.

e. [Brand Identity]: Discuss the importance of creating a consistent brand identity on social media platforms. Provide tips for developing a brand voice and visual identity that resonates with the target audience.

f. [Engagement Strategies]: Provide strategies for improving engagement on social media platforms, such as responding to comments, hosting contests, and sharing user-generated content.

g. [Social Media Metrics]: Discuss key social media metrics and their significance, such as engagement rate, reach, and conversion rate. Provide strategies for tracking and analyzing these metrics to measure social media performance and effectiveness.

h. [Influencer Collaboration]: Discuss the benefits and challenges of working with influencers on social media platforms, and provide strategies for identifying and collaborating with the right influencers for a business.

i. [Social Media Advertising]: Discuss best practices

for creating and managing paid social media campaigns, including targeting, budgeting, and ad creatives.

j. [Platform-Specific Strategies]: Discuss the unique features and challenges of different social media platforms, such as Facebook, Instagram, Twitter, and LinkedIn. Provide platform-specific strategies for effective content creation and engagement.

10. **Crisis Management: Offering advice on navigating and resolving social media crises, including addressing negative feedback and mitigating potential damage.**

a. [Social Media Monitoring]: Discuss the importance of social media monitoring and how it can help detect and prevent potential crises. Provide examples of tools and strategies for effective social media monitoring.

b. [Engaging with Customers]: Discuss the importance of engaging with customers on social media and how it can impact brand reputation and loyalty. Provide examples of effective customer engagement strategies.

c. [Creating Engaging Content]: Discuss the key elements of creating engaging social media content, such as visuals, storytelling, and authenticity. Provide examples of successful campaigns and how they used these elements.

d. [Incorporating Video Content]: Discuss the

benefits of incorporating video content into social media strategies and best practices for creating and promoting videos on different platforms.

e. [Innovative Campaigns]: Discuss innovative social media campaigns and how they can differentiate a brand in a crowded market. Provide examples of successful campaigns and how they were executed.

f. [Building a Social Media Team]: Discuss the skills and roles needed for a successful social media team and how to effectively manage and collaborate with team members.

g. [Measuring Success]: Discuss the importance of measuring social media success and the key metrics to track, such as engagement, reach, and conversions. Provide examples of how to analyze and interpret social media data.

h. [Social Media Ethics]: Discuss the ethical considerations in social media management, such as privacy, transparency, and responsibility. Provide examples of how to uphold ethical standards in social media practices.

i. [Targeting the Right Audience]: Discuss the importance of targeting the right audience on social media and how to use demographics, interests, and behaviors to create targeted campaigns. Provide examples of successful campaigns that effectively targeted a specific audience.

j. [Incorporating User-Generated Content]: Discuss the benefits of incorporating user-generated content into social media strategies and how to encourage and manage user-generated content. Provide examples of successful campaigns that incorporated user-generated content.